D1082868

# THE
# AGINCOURT
## COMPANION

# THE
# AGINCOURT
## COMPANION

A guide to the legendary battle and
warfare in the medieval world

Anne Curry
Peter Hoskins
Thom Richardson
Dan Spencer

ANDRE
DEUTSCH

THIS IS AN ANDRE DEUTSCH BOOK

Published in 2015 by André Deutsch Limited
A division of the Carlton Publishing Group
20 Mortimer Street
London W1T 3JW

10 9 8 7 6 5 4 3 2 1

Text © Anne Curry, Peter Hoskins, Thom Richardson and Dan Spencer
Design © André Deutsch Limited 2015

A catalogue record for this book is available from the British Library

ISBN 978 0 233 00471 6

Printed in Dubai

# CONTENTS

# INTRODUCTION

The 600th anniversary of the Battle of Agincourt falls on 25 October 2015. On this day in 1415, Henry V gained a great victory over the French close to the modern-day village of Azincourt, which lies approximately 45 miles (75km) south of Calais. Henry had invaded in the middle of August to pursue his claims in France, capturing the town of Harfleur by 22 September, but was intercepted and engaged in battle with the French as he marched his army across northern France.

War between England and France was nothing new. English kings had held lands in France ever since Duke William of Normandy (better known to us as William the Conqueror) had defeated Harold II at the Battle of Hastings in 1066. Although his great grandson, the equally famous, if less applauded King John had lost the duchy of Normandy in 1204, he and his successors continued to hold lands inherited from Eleanor of Aquitaine, wife of Henry II, in south-west France, focusing on the city of Bordeaux. These possessions generated centuries of conflict with the kings of France. In 1328, this conflict deepened. Following the death of the French king Charles IV on 1 February of that year, his nearest heir was his sister Isabella of France's son, Edward III, King of England. Even though the French disregarded his claim, insisting on male-only descent, Edward III and his successors never gave up on the potential value of their claim to stir up trouble. The result was the Hundred Years War.

From 1340 onwards, save for a brief period of peace in the 1360s, successive kings of England also claimed sovereignty over the French throne. Thus, it was as King of France that

Henry V invaded in 1415, seeking to recover lost rights by conquering the duchy of Normandy, an audacious move, which strained every sinew of his English crown. Henry's army was one of the largest raised in late medieval England, a huge component of which was the already famous English (and Welsh) archers. These archers contributed greatly to the battle's success. This was Henry's moment: the French were already divided among themselves; they were engaged in civil war and ruled by a mentally unstable king.

*The Agincourt Companion* is a commemorative journey, focusing on the events of 1415. Here, we set the scene for Henry's invasion of France, chart his progress from the taxing siege of Harfleur and his anxious march across France to his ultimate victory at Agincourt. The battle itself was a bloody and morale-sapping defeat for the French and Henry's archers were largely to thank for this. In tribute to the archers' crucial role at Agincourt, it gives us great pleasure to dedicate the royalties of this book to The Fletchers Trust which supports Team GB Paralympic Archers.

–Anne Curry, Peter Hoskins, Thom Richardson and Dan Spencer

# 1

# THE HUNDRED
# YEARS WAR

 ## THE ORIGIN OF THE NAME
## "HUNDRED YEARS WAR"

The "Hundred Years War" is the term given to a period of conflict between England and France stretching from 1337 until 1453. It began with the confiscation by the French king Philip VI of the English-held duchy of Aquitaine, and ended with the final expulsion of the English from all of their French possessions (save Calais). The name, introduced by French historians in the early nineteenth century as a convenient way to describe this era in Anglo–French hostilities, was taken up by British historians and is now widely used.

The period was by no means the first time the English and French had been at war. From the late twelfth century onwards, there were disputes over the lands held by English kings in France. In 1328, a new element entered the equation – the French Crown itself. Charles IV of France died without a direct male heir. His nearest relative was his nephew Edward III, King of England and Duke of Aquitaine, whose claim was through his mother, Queen Isabella, sister of Charles IV. But the French were hardly likely to choose him as their king. Instead, they claimed that the Crown could only pass through male descent, and that therefore the rightful king was Philip, Count of Valois, who became Philip VI. At first, Edward III had little choice but to acquiesce, but when Anglo–French relations deteriorated in the 1330s, he was able to raise the question of his claim again. In 1340, he formally declared himself King of France. The Hundred Years War is therefore the term applied to the wars of the fourteenth and fifteenth centuries in which English kings claimed the throne of France. This claim continued even after their French lands were lost. Not until 1801 was it given up.

Both England and France involved themselves in internal disputes, such as the war of succession in the duchy of Brittany in the mid-fourteenth century and the French civil war between the Burgundians and Armagnacs in the early fifteenth century. The Hundred Years War also involved other areas of Europe. The English were particularly keen to have the Flemish as their allies since the county of Flanders lay within the kingdom of France and was England's main market for wool. The Scots were an important ally of the French ever since they had fought against Edward I's attempts to control the kingdom of Scotland in the 1290s. The Franco–Scottish alliance (often called "the Auld Alliance") persisted for the duration of the Hundred Years War.

 THE PLANTAGENET INHERITANCE

English kings had long-standing interests in France, dating back to 1066 when William, Duke of Normandy, invaded England and defeated Harold Godwinson at the Battle of Hastings. From this date until 1453, kings of England were holders of substantial lands in France, which invariably led to tension with the kings of France. This rivalry was intensified by the massive territorial acquisition of lands that occurred during the reign of King Henry II of England (r.1154–89). Henry had inherited the counties of Anjou, Maine, and Touraine from his father, Geoffrey Plantagenet, and the duchy of Normandy from his mother, Matilda (daughter of Henry I of England). His marriage to Eleanor of Aquitaine, in 1152, led to his obtaining the duchy of Aquitaine, which at that time incorporated most of south-western France.

The acquisition of such substantial territories in France meant that much of Henry II's reign, and that of his sons and successors, Richard I (r.1189–99) and John (r.1199–1216), was marked by conflict with Philip Augustus (Philip II), King of France. The latter was able to skilfully exploit divisions among the Plantagenet family and encourage rebellions in their diverse lands, which led to the loss of Normandy, Anjou and Maine during the reign of King John. The northern part of the duchy of Aquitaine, the county of Poitou focused on Poitiers, was lost to the French in 1224. This meant that the possessions of the English Crown in France were limited to a reduced duchy of Aquitaine.

In the Treaty of Paris of 1259, made between Louis IX of France and Henry III of England, the English finally accepted the loss of the northern lands in return for confirmation of the lands they held in Aquitaine. In 1279, the county of Ponthieu centered on the mouth of the river Somme also came into the hands of the English Crown through the inheritance of Edward I's queen, Eleanor of Castile. But these lands were not held outright. The King of England had to pay homage to the King of France for them. The Treaty of Paris had confirmed this situation, which became increasingly unsatisfactory as the theoretical and actual powers of kings increased in the late thirteenth and early fourteenth centuries. It was demeaning for the King of England to have to kneel before his French overlord and pay homage. All the advantages seemed to lie with the French.

The King of France had rights of overlordship over the English-held lands. If the English king was seen to contravene these the former had the right to confiscate the lands. The French were keen to stir up trouble by encouraging the local population to send in appeals against the English. War broke out in 1294–98 and again in 1324, which led to a further reduction in the size of the territory. By the time of Edward III's ascension to the throne, in January 1327, English control in Aquitaine was largely limited to the region of Gascony (also known as Guyenne) based upon the cities of Bordeaux and Bayonne.

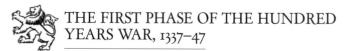

## THE FIRST PHASE OF THE HUNDRED YEARS WAR, 1337–47

At the outset of his reign, Edward III's youth and political instability in England made it impossible for him to press his claim to the French throne. He was forced to give homage to Philip VI in 1329. Over the course of the 1330s, relations worsened, especially as Philip supported David II, the exiled king of Scotland who had been disinherited by Edward's nominee, Edward Balliol. This situation was made more tense by the presence in England of Robert of Artois, a French nobleman in dispute with Philip VI. Edward III, who also held the French title Duke of Aquitaine, was asked to hand the nobleman over to Philip. When he refused, the French king confiscated the duchy of Aquitaine on 24 May 1337 and sent an army into the territory.

Aquitaine was the cause of war between England and France, yet most of the fighting of the first phase of the Hundred Years War occurred in the north of France. Edward III negotiated military alliances with many of the rulers of the Low Countries in 1337. In return for hefty English subsidies, they agreed to provide large numbers of soldiers for an invasion of northern France. The eventual attack, which occurred in 1339, resulted in an inconclusive stand off, however. In the following year, Edward entered into an alliance with the townsmen who were in rebellion against the Count of Flanders, a vassal and close supporter of the French king. In part to provide legitimacy for his new allies, Edward III formally declared himself King of France at Ghent on 26 January 1340, adopting the quartered arms of the fleur-de-lys of France and the leopards of England. The English scored a notable naval victory at Sluys on 24 June 1340 but failed in the effort to take Tournai from the French for the benefit of their Flemish allies. Following the death of John III, Duke of Brittany, in 1341, the war spread to north-west France in the succeeding years, with the French and English backing rival claimants to the duchy.

In July 1346, Edward invaded Normandy with a large army. After attacking the city of Caen by storm, the English marched east towards Paris in an attempt to bring Philip VI to battle. Heading north into Edward's county of Ponthieu, they engaged in battle at Crécy on 26 August against a French royal army led in person by Philip VI. This was the first major battle of the war and resulted in an English victory. The archers were able to inflict particular havoc on the mounted French men-at-arms, which served as a powerful demonstration of the lethality of the longbow. This victory added greatly to the prestige of Edward III and meant that the French were more wary about engaging in battle with him in the future. After Crécy, the English marched north towards the strategic town of Calais, which they besieged. The townspeople were eventually forced to surrender after a siege of almost a year; thereafter it served as a useful bridgehead for future English expeditions to France.

 ## THE BLACK PRINCE

In the 1350s, the focus of the war shifted back to Aquitaine and to campaigns in south-west France. Edward III sent his eldest son, the Prince of Wales, Edward of Woodstock (more commonly known in later centuries as the "Black Prince") to Bordeaux with a small army in 1355. He launched a raid eastwards into the Languedoc, causing much destruction.

In the following year, Edward III came up an ambitious scheme to invade France with three separate armies led by himself from Calais, the Black Prince from the south and Henry of Grosmont,

Duke of Lancaster, from the north. In the event, the king's army remained in England in the face of a threat from Scotland. The prince's Anglo–Gascon army was intercepted at Poitiers by an army led by John II, King of France. This resulted in another major victory for the English on 19 September 1356, made all the more important by the capture of the French king himself, who was then taken to England. Possession of the King of France meant that Edward had a powerful negotiating tool with the French; it also contributed to the breakdown of royal authority across much of France. Bands of soldiers professing loyalty to Edward III, called *routiers*, ranged across large parts of France terrorizing the local populations. Major rebellions also broke out in northern France in Paris and in the countryside.

 THE TREATY OF BRÉTIGNY, 1360

After the capture of John II, negotiations for settlement began in earnest but the French refused to meet Edward's terms. In 1359, Edward again invaded France aiming to take the traditional French crowning place of Reims and to proclaim himself king. This campaign failed and he instead agreed to a peace settlement. The Treaty of Brétigny, agreed on 25 May 1360, was very favourable to Edward because he held the trump card of John II as his prisoner. In return for John II's release, the French agreed to cede in full sovereignty extensive lands in south-west France; this almost restored the whole of the old duchy of Aquitaine, Calais and Ponthieu to Edward, who also received a huge ransom for King John of three million *écus*. In return, Edward agreed to put aside his French royal title, but this did not matter as he had gained so much territory in France for which he was no longer obliged to pay homage. As a symbol of this, he began to call himself "Lord" rather than "Duke" of Aquitaine.

Edward III was therefore undoubtedly the victor of the war that occurred from 1337 to 1360. The territories under his control were significantly augmented and his coffers were swelled by the ransom money, so much so that he did not need to raise direct taxation in England in the following years. In 1362, Edward proclaimed his son and heir, Edward of Woodstock, Prince of Aquitaine with vice-regal powers over the enlarged duchy. Subsequently, the prince became involved in the civil war in Castile between Peter II and Henry of Trastámara. He led a large Anglo–Gascon army across the Pyrenees, which defeated Trastámara, along with his French allies, at the Battle of Nájera on 3 April 1367. This proved to be a pyrrhic victory, however, as Peter refused to honour his financial promises to Prince Edward, which led to severe financial problems in the principality. In disgust, the Black Prince abandoned his ally, who was later defeated and killed by Trastámara. A significant decline in the Black Prince's health coincided with rising tensions with Charles V, King of France. War broke out again in 1369.

 THE RESUMPTION OF WAR, 1369–96

Charles V (r.1364–80) was able to exploit loopholes in the Treaty of Brétigny to reclaim, in 1369, French feudal authority over English lands in France. Edward III was unprepared for the reopening of war. He began calling himself King of France once more but the resumption of hostilities was marked by a swift French campaign that focused on taking towns and castles and which reversed almost all of his earlier gains. French armies were able to overrun much of the duchy of Aquitaine in the south-west and the county of Ponthieu in the north. Successive English armies were sent to France but they failed to turn the tide of war. Edward III died in 1377 and was succeeded by his 10-year-old grandson, Richard II (r.1377–99) – Richard's father, Edward the Black Prince, had died the previous year.

By the mid-1380s, the English were in a dangerous situation, at war with France, Scotland, Castile and Flanders (the latter having fallen under French royal control thanks to the marriage of its heiress, Margaret of Flanders, to one of the sons of John II). This situation encouraged the French to attempt two major invasions of England in the years 1385 and 1386, the first linked to a simultaneous invasion from the north by a Franco–Scottish army. This contributed to political instability in England in 1387, when Richard II was almost deposed by a coalition of disgruntled noblemen called the Lords Appellant, who condemned some of his closest supporters to death.

Richard was later able to reassert his authority in England but recognized that some sort of settlement with France had to be reached. In March 1396, the Truce of Leulinghen was agreed, whereby both kingdoms would be at peace for 28 years and Richard would marry Charles's daughter, Isabella. By this point, English possessions in France were limited to the coastal area of Aquitaine between Bordeaux and Bayonne with a small inland extension along the Dordogne, and also to Calais and its surrounding area.

 RICHARD II AND HENRY IV

In 1397, Richard took action against his domestic political opponents. This included the executions of prominent noblemen, notably his uncle Thomas of Woodstock, Duke of Gloucester and Richard, Earl of Arundel. In the following year, he temporarily exiled his cousin, Henry Bolingbroke, Duke of Hereford, the son of his uncle, John of Gaunt, Duke of Lancaster. Gaunt died in 1399, but Richard would not allow Bolingbroke to return from exile to sue for his inheritance. The absence of the king on a military expedition to Ireland in the same year, however, gave Bolingbroke an opportunity to invade England. He was quickly able to secure control over the country. Richard was captured and forced to abdicate in September 1399.

The failure of a plot in January 1400 to restore Richard to the throne, hatched by supporters of the deposed king, led to Henry's decision to have him killed. The French interpreted Henry IV's usurpation of the throne as a hostile act. Despite the official continuation of the truce, the breakdown in relations led to French attacks on Aquitaine and Calais in the first decade of the fifteenth century. The French also provided support for the Scots and for the Welsh rebels under Owain Glyndŵr. However, as the first decade of the fifteenth century came to an end, Henry IV had secured his position in England, while the French were in turmoil as a result of the insanity of their king, Charles VI.

 ## CHARLES VI'S MADNESS AND THE FRENCH CIVIL WAR

In August 1392, while riding in the forest neat Le Mans, Charles VI (r.1380–1422) was afflicted by a bout of madness and attacked members of his entourage. Over the following years, until his death in 1422, he suffered from periodic episodes of insanity. This meant that his ability to rule was severely curtailed and a power struggle over the kingdom ensued between his relatives. Rivalry between Louis, Duke of Orléans, brother of the king, and John the Fearless, Duke of Burgundy, culminated in the murder of Louis by assassins working under the direction of John in November 1407. By 1410, there was open war between the Burgundian and Orléanist (usually called Armagnac since Louis's heir Charles married the daughter of the count of Armagnac) factions. Attempts at reconciliation by Charles VI, during his periods of lucidity, proved to be unsuccessful. This civil war in France meant that the kingdom was vulnerable to outside interference, which both English kings Henry IV and Henry V were keen to exploit.

# 2

# HENRY V

## THE LANCASTRIAN DYNASTY

Edmund "Crouchback", the son of Henry III (r.1216–72) and younger brother of Edward I (r.1272–1307), became Earl of Lancaster in 1267: this collateral line of the royal family formed the Lancastrian dynasty. Edmund was succeeded as earl by his son Thomas in 1296, who became prominent in opposition to Edward II and was defeated, captured and executed by royal forces at the Battle of Boroughbridge on 16 March 1322. His brother Henry successfully petitioned Edward for restitution of the earldom in 1324 but then supported the queen and Roger Mortimer in their deposition of the king. At Henry's death in 1345, he was succeeded by his son, another Henry, who was prominent in the French wars of Edward III, especially in the Aquitaine theatre, as well as being one of the founding knights of the Order of the Garter. In March 1350, he was created Duke of Lancaster.

However, at Henry's death on 24 March 1361, he left no male heir only two daughters, between whom his inheritance was divided according to the customary practice in the case of co-heiresses. The eldest daughter, Maud, died without issue in 1362. Therefore all of the inheritance devolved upon her younger sister, Blanche, who was born *c.* 1347. She had already married John of Gaunt, the third son of Edward III, who so called because he had been born in Ghent in 1340 shortly after his father had declared himself King of France in that town in order to gain the support of the Flemish.

On 13 November 1362, following the death of Maud, his sister-in-law, John of Gaunt was created Duke of Lancaster. He joined his elder brother, Edward of Woodstock (the Black Prince) in his Spanish campaigns of the 1360s in support of Pedro II against his French-backed half-brother, Henry of Trastámara, and was present at the victory at Nájera on 3 April 1367.

When the war with France restarted in 1369, John was appointed royal lieutenant and led several campaigns, including a great chevauchée (see pages 109–10) from Calais to Bordeaux in 1373. In subsequent years, he gained a personal stake in international affairs through his second marriage to Constance, heiress of Pedro II, in 1371. This led to his assumption of the style "King of Castile and Léon" by right of his wife and to his involvement in campaigns in Castile in the 1380s against Trastámara (who had murdered Pedro and, with French backing, had succeeded in becoming king). When peace was brokered through the marriage of the daughter of John and Constance to Henry's son, Gaunt was compensated by Richard II with the grant of the duchy of Aquitaine.

In England, Gaunt was prominent (but not always popular) for his role in the minority of Richard II. He remained a significant figure throughout the reign, not least because his duchy of Lancaster, along with subordinate titles, was a huge landholding whose tentacles stretched across many parts of England and Wales. During the troubled politics of Richard's reign, Gaunt's son, Henry Bolingbroke, fell out of favour with the king and was sent into exile for 10 years in 1398. In response to Richard's refusal to let him return at the death of his father in 1399, he invaded and deposed Richard, taking the throne as Henry IV, the first Lancastrian king.

HENRY OF MONMOUTH

Although Bolingbroke's eldest son, the future Henry V (r.1413–22), was never called Henry of Monmouth during his lifetime, he was certainly born in the castle of Monmouth on 16 September 1386. It was owned by his grandfather John of Gaunt as part of the great Lancastrian landholdings. At this point, the young Lord Henry was heir to his grandfather's title and lands and also stood to inherit part of the great Bohun inheritance from his mother, Mary de Bohun. Therefore, at the time, he was an important nobleman, enjoying significant political, social and economic power in England. However, his life was transformed following his father's usurpation of Richard II. Henry became Prince of Wales, Earl of Chester, Duke of Cornwall – and also Duke of Aquitaine and Duke of Lancaster for good measure.

Prince Henry shared in the political upheavals of his father's reign. A usurper was always subject to challenge and in Henry IV's case this was all the more so as he was not the heir apparent of Richard II. Henry was descended from the third son of Edward III but Lionel, Duke of Clarence (d. 1361), Edward's second son, had descendants, the Mortimers. Their claim came through the female line – Lionel's only child, his daughter, Philippa. However, if the English right to France was through a woman, there was no legal reason why the Mortimer claim was not equally valid. However, the Mortimers were at a disadvantage because in 1399, their heir apparent, Edmund, was only eight years old.

The early years of Henry IV's reign were particularly troubled. In the autumn of 1400, a revolt broke out in Wales under Owain Glyndŵr, who assumed the title Prince of Wales. Worse still was the threat of joint action between Edmund Mortimer's uncle, who had defected to Glyndŵr after being captured by him, and the Percy family, the earls of Northumberland, who had originally supported the Lancastrian usurpation but had become disaffected with the new king. On 21 July 1403, Prince Henry, then 16 years old, was entrusted with command of the vanguard in the Battle of Shrewsbury against Sir Henry Percy (Hotspur) who had raised rebellion. During this royal victory the prince was wounded by an arrow to his face, though a skilful operation removed the barb and he lived on to continue the war in Wales.

By 1409, King Henry IV's health was in decline and Prince Henry became more closely involved with government. Expecting his father to die soon, the prince became increasingly frustrated at having to wait to become king. For much of 1410 and 1411, he was in effective control of government because Henry IV was physically incapacitated. It was at this point that the matter of France started to become very influential in English politics. Charles VI was mentally ill and was unable to rule France.

 PRELUDE TO WAR: 1411–12

In France, King Charles VI was incapacitated due to the mental illness that had begun as early as 1392. This had caused a fight between rival factions for control of both the king and government. By 1410, the Burgundian and Armagnac parties were moving towards civil war. Both sides sought military aid from the English against their enemies, offering in return promises of support for English claims to lands in France.

While Prince Henry was in control of his father's government, he supported the Burgundians. Although he did not come to a full treaty with John the Fearless, Duke of Burgundy, in 1411 he sent troops led by his close friend Thomas, Earl of Arundel. They helped the Burgundians win a victory at St Cloud on 9 November 1411. We cannot be sure how many English troops were sent, but chroniclers cite figures between 1,200 and 2,600 men. Some of the commanders, such as Gilbert Umfraville and John Phelip, also served on the 1415 expedition, as did the Earl of Arundel. Another Englishman, Sir John Oldcastle was also involved. Part of Prince Henry's circle, he subsequently attracted the attention of Church leaders for his Lollard beliefs and, in 1413, Henry, now king had no choice but to hand him over for trial as a heretic.

In November 1411, Henry IV had recovered enough to take back direct control of government, effectively sacking the prince and his supporters in the royal council. The king was also persuaded by the blandishments of the Armagnac lords – the Dukes of Berry, Bourbon, and Orléans; the Count of Alençon; and the Lords of Albret and Armagnac – to come to a deal with them against the Burgundians. Their strategy was to promise more to the king than Duke John of Burgundy had done.

In the Treaty of Bourges, ratified in London on 18 May 1412, the Armagnac lords recognized the right of Henry IV to the whole of the duchy of Aquitaine in full sovereignty and offered to assist him in his "just quarrels". In return, Henry promised to provide 1,000 men-at-arms and 3,000 archers to support the Armagnacs against the Burgundians. At this point, Duke John of Burgundy was controlling Charles VI and the royal government and the Armagnacs were essentially rebelling against their own king. They had no authority to make any promises at all to Henry IV and the English expedition achieved nothing since not long after it landed, the two factions made their peace. But clearly, Henry IV had seen potential advantages in stirring up trouble in France.

In reality, though the 1412 expedition stirred up more trouble in England. Prince Henry was extremely annoyed that his next eldest brother, Thomas (created Duke of Clarence at this very point) was given command of the 4,000-strong English army. He also suffered a loss of face in Europe when he had to apologize to the Duke of Burgundy for the complete change of policy, explaining that he had no choice because his father had decided to assist the Armagnacs. Their differences of opinion over foreign policy were the main reason for the breakdown of relations between Prince Henry and his father. The situation reached crisis point in the summer of 1412, when the king suspected that his eldest son was intending to stage a coup. Although there were acts of reconciliation, it remains uncertain as to whether father and son were ever truly reunited.

# THE NEW KING

Henry V finally came to the throne on 21 March 1413, after his father's death. Aged 25, he had been awaiting this moment for some time. He took his new role and responsibilities very seriously. Indeed, several contemporary writers note how he consciously changed his persona. Gone were the princely vices, vanquished by Henry's religious and moral conversion, which transformed him into the model of kingship. In the early years of his reign, he sought to ensure law and order, to take advice from only the most upright of men and to effect strong and "hands-on" kingship. Such actions point to the likely truth of stories of a misspent youth, so entertainingly portrayed by Shakespeare's Hal in *Henry IV Parts 1 and 2*. Henry's religiosity is an important element in this transformation. We see it in his monastic foundations, the last established before the Reformation, and in his support for the suppression of heresy, especially following the abortive Lollard rising of January 1414 led by his former friend, Sir John Oldcastle.

How did France fit into this? The truce needed to be renewed at every change of ruler. Initially the French made this heavy going. Henry's reputation in Europe was not good. The sending of tennis balls by the dauphin – as portrayed in Shakespeare's *Henry V* – symbolizes the lack of regard for Henry's military and political reputation and is almost certainly true. However, whether it occurred in the spring of 1414 or the following year remains unclear. As a new king, Henry was keen to prove himself at home and abroad. He had already tried to play his hand in 1411 when he supported the Duke of Burgundy. By the time Henry's envoys arrived in France to negotiate the renewal of the truce, it was obvious that relations between the Burgundian and Armagnac factions were worsening. Duke John of Burgundy lost his control over the king. By February 1414, he had been declared a traitor and his erstwhile enemies were soon making open war on his lands in Picardy and Artois. Charles VI was now under the control of his eldest son, the dauphin Louis, and the Armagnacs.

It is hardly surprising that Henry hoped to take advantage of the civil war in France. We also see quite early in his reign that he was keen on a marriage to Princess Catherine, daughter of Charles VI of France, especially if it carried a large dowry from her father. As the civil war in France heightened, so Henry increased his pressure. A great embassy sent to France in the autumn of 1414 was given powers to discuss two means of coming to a full peace settlement: through marriage and through the restoration of English rights – in other words, the lands given to Edward III in the Treaty of Brétigny of 1360. We see here Henry wanting to make his mark by sorting out the dispute with France once and for all. But at the same time Henry engaged in negotiations with Burgundy to keep the pressure on the French royal government.

 INVASION PLANS

By the late autumn of 1414, Henry V was obsessed by relations with France. Having sent a large embassy – the first major Anglo–French negotiations since the mid-1390s – he could not afford to lose face. Therefore, at the same time, he raised the prospect of a significant invasion of France. No king had led an expedition to the Continent in person since Edward III had invaded in 1359, with the aim of taking the coronation city of Reims and making himself king. In the end, Henry turned instead to negotiating the advantageous terms of the Treaty of Brétigny.

Henry V's ambition was to make his mark either by diplomacy or war or, if necessary, both. The moment seemed right. As the chancellor announced at the opening of parliament on 19 November 1414, it was a suitable time for the king to achieve his purpose. Divisions in France made an invasion all the more attractive. His lords and knights expressed a willingness to give him the military support he sought, although they also urged him to send another embassy to France.

By the time his ambassadors arrived in Paris in early March

1415, the French factions had made their peace. Therefore they simply dismissed Henry's diplomatic approaches and he had no choice but to proceed with his preparations for war – although we can imagine that this was not to his displeasure, but very much the opposite.

In fact some preparations had already begun in February, such as orders for the production of tents. On 10 March, Henry summoned the mayor and aldermen of London to the Tower of London to tell them of his intention to invade France: this was the first stage of negotiations with the City for a loan to support his endeavour. Preparations moved on apace and with some interesting effects. On 14 April, for instance, Henry ordered a proclamation in London that the price of arms and armour should be lowered: clearly the king did not want the London armourers to use the opportunity of increased demand to feather their own nests.

By the end of April, Henry negotiated with the nobility, knights, gentry and others for the provision of troops within the indenture system. Most indentures were sealed on 29 April. All told, about 320 men, some acting jointly, promised to provide troops. Henry intended to make a large showing in France with between 11 and 12,000 men. The indentures were for a year-long campaign. This, as well as the recruitment of miners, stonemasons, carpenters, labourers, etc, confirms that Henry's intention was for a campaign of conquest. Although he had maintained a subterfuge to confuse the French that he might be heading for Gascony, he had already decided on Normandy as his target. It was easily accessible from England and was a rich area whose conquest would bring many benefits including damaging the power and resources of the French Crown.

Henry moved down to Winchester in early June. Although a last-minute French embassy was sent to England, the die had been cast. Troops started arriving in the Southampton area in early July. The expedition set sail to Normandy on about 11 August. This was later than Henry had planned. His departure had been delayed by a plot against his life.

# THE SOUTHAMPTON PLOT

There were undoubted anxieties about the security of the realm during the king's proposed expedition to France. Troops had been sent to Wales and the Scottish borders, for instance, in case those areas took advantage of the king's absence to cause difficulties. But no one anticipated that there would be a plot within the royal circle to depose the king in favour of his cousin Edmund Mortimer, Earl of March. This plot was revealed to the king by Edmund himself on 31 July and led to the immediate arrest of the alleged conspirators, their trial and execution.

The plotters were Richard, Earl of Cambridge, another cousin of Henry V, who was descended from the fourth son of Edward III and was the brother of Edward, Duke of York; Sir Thomas Grey of Heton, a Northumberland knight who added a Scottish element to the plot; and Henry, Lord Scrope of Masham, whose offence was knowing about but not disclosing the revolt to the king. Grey was hung drawn and quartered on 2 August and the two peers were beheaded on 5 August.

The exact reasons for the plot remain obscure. Both March and Cambridge were annoyed with the king's demands for high marriage fines but this seems a small matter to lead to their alleged crime. Scrope was accused of being in the pay of the French. He had certainly been in France as a royal envoy in the past.

What is really significant is that the plot was planned for the very moment Henry was preparing to embark and when he had a large number of troops in his company in the Southampton area. This suggests that the plotters considered there might be others who were not keen on the expedition. A Frenchman, later tried in Paris for spying for the English, claimed at his trial that there were many in England who favoured Thomas, Duke of Clarence, Henry's next eldest brother (who had been his father's favourite, too) or the Earl of March. Henry's swift move against the plotters showed that he would not be deflected from his plan to invade France.

# 3

# RAISING THE ARMY

 ## THE INDENTURE SYSTEM

The army that Henry V took to France in 1415 was paid for its services. This had been the case throughout the Hundred Years War. An important development from 1369 onwards was the dominance of the indenture system. Before this date, indentures (essentially contracts written out twice and cut across the middle in a way that resembled teeth – a means of avoiding fraud) had been used for appointments to garrison commands and for some expeditions where the king was not present in person. After 1369, they were used for all expeditions. Therefore, while the indentures for 1415 may appear complex, they were based on a long-standing precedent that allowed the king to raise an army in a well-organized manner easy to monitor in financial terms. This was a period in which royal accountants were as crucial to the war effort as soldiers. Usefully, too, the indenture system placed the responsibility for recruiting the troops on those who entered into a contract with the Crown. We could even see this as a form of privatization.

Most of the indentures for the 1415 campaign were sealed in Westminster on 29 April 1415. Before this date, there had already been discussion as early as November 1414 between the king and his nobles and gentry on how many men each of them might be able to and, indeed, be expected to provide. Generally, retinue sizes followed social status. The two biggest retinues were to be provided by the king's brothers, the Duke of Clarence with 960 men, the Duke of Gloucester with 800 and the other royal duke, York, contracting for 400 men. Earls provided companies of between 120 and 220 men, but Henry's half-uncle, the Earl of Dorset, and his close friend the Earl of Arundel were significant enough to offer 400 men. Knights commonly indented for between 400 and 120 men and esquires 12 or so. Many who indented for the campaign offered very small companies or even simply service in person.

Henry cast the recruitment net wide, including even the domestic servants of the royal household. In reality, the large retinues of dukes and earls were made up of many small groups, with some men acting as sub-contractors and bringing along troops to contribute to the retinue as a whole. For the earls of Salisbury and Dorset, some of these sub-indentures survive in the royal records.

Around 320 men entered into indentures, although several did so as a group rather than as individuals. Not all indentures survive in the records of the Exchequer, but where they are missing we can reconstruct the numbers for which men contracted thanks to the warrants for issue (orders to pay men) and the issue rolls (which record all royal expenditure). Indentures were generally in standard form and followed past precedents. So, for instance, they offered standard rates of pay: 6d per day for an archer, one shilling per day for a man-at-arms, two shillings per day for a knight bachelor, four shillings per day for a knight banneret and a baron, 6s 8d for an earl, and 13s 4d for a duke. Those who indented did so for a whole 12 months, confirming the fact that Henry intended a long campaign of conquest.

The pay for two quarters (i.e. the first six months) was to be paid in advance, following standard practice for year-long campaigns. Unusually, however, only the first quarter was to be paid in cash. For the second quarter, Henry gave items from the royal jewel collection to those who entered into contracts to serve on the campaign as security for future payment and arrangements were in place for the third and fourth quarters on the assumption that the campaign would be successful and Henry would gain access to further funds. (Some of the indentures were worded to include a possible campaign in Gascony, where higher wage rates were payable, but this was most likely to keep the French guessing as to Henry's intentions.) The indentures also outlined terms and conditions, such as the sharing out of war profits, including ransoms. They also anticipated that troops should be ready to muster at the coast on 1 July. The king agreed to provide shipping.

Almost all companies were intended to be made up of men-at-arms and archers in a ratio of 1:3. This was a contrast with the late fourteenth-century expeditions to France where a ratio of 1:1 was common. Henry was keen to raise as large an army as possible and archers were easier to recruit as well as being cheaper. The troops raised by indentures with the nobles, knights and gentry were boosted by the recruitment of special archer companies from South Wales (500), Lancashire (500) and Cheshire (650), commanded by small numbers of men-at-arms. In addition, we see support staff, such as miners, carpenters, smiths, stone masons and so on. Since there would also have been pages and other household staff, numbers actually crossing to France were very large, as were the numbers of horses the army took with them. The Earl Marshal for example had 24 horses, while the knights of his company had six each. Most men-at-arms took two horses, and archers one apiece.

 ## THE RETINUE OF JOHN MOWBRAY, EARL MARSHAL

John Mowbray, Earl Marshal and Earl of Nottingham (1392– 1432) was about 23 at the time of the 1415 expedition. Although he was invalided home on 5 October, just before the English army left Harfleur for the march to Calais, he recovered and served

Henry V on later expeditions. He played a prominent role in the French wars until his death in 1432, being created Duke of Norfolk in 1425. While he was absent from England in 1415, his wife, Katherine Neville (daughter of the Earl of Westmorland), gave birth to his son and heir, John, on 12 September.

On 29 April 1415, Earl John indented to provide 200 soldiers, who, in addition to himself, comprised four knights bachelor, 45 men-at-arms and 150 archers. On 6 June, he received the first instalment of pay, being half of what was due for the first quarter of service. The second instalment was debited at the Exchequer on 6 July and paid to the earl as he mustered. For the second quarter, he was given royal jewels worth over £723 in June.

When Earl John's final account was dealt with at the Exchequer in May 1423, his representative, John Fishlake, presented a list which gave details of the fate of the retinue on the campaign, showing that 138 had been at the battle, but that 12 men-at-arms and 45 archers had been invalided home with the earl. These men are also named in a list of sick, since Henry was very keen to know whose pay to stop after the first quarter! We also have a list of the earl's men in the so-called "Agincourt roll", a partial copy made in the late sixteenth century of a now-lost Exchequer list of men present at the battle.

Thanks to the survival of the account of the earl's receiver-general for the financial year 29 September 1414 to 28 September 1415, we can tell more about the earl's soldiers and about his preparations for the campaign. We can see that he had to borrow 1,000 marks from the Earl of Arundel, along with smaller loans from the prior and monks of Thetford Priory and the rector of Southfield to help him with his high costs. This was his first military expedition and he had only gained control of his lands two years earlier.

The earl needed to buy a new "cote armour" as well as a trapper for his horse, both woven with his arms as Earl Marshal. A mainsail for his ship and a number of other flags were also required, as was a tent for his stable. An old tent was repaired for use as his garderobe. A new iron seat was purchased for his latrine, as well as a bed and mattress, and items for his chapel, which accompanied him on the campaign. A number of medications were also bought, although clearly the "electura against the flux" (dysentery) did not prove as efficacious as he had hoped. Food and drink were prepared for use on the campaign, and we can also see that additional victuals were sent to him during the siege of Harfleur.

As for his troops, the earl's receiver-general's account shows two major points. The first is that the earl's retinue was in reality made up of lots of small companies. Sir Thomas Rokeby provided one man-at-arms and nine archers, Sir Nicholas Colfox two men-at-arms and seven archers. Perceval Lyndley, esquire, brought along six men-at-arms and 15 archers (and he was to see himself knighted during the campaign). Eleven men-at-arms brought two archers, but 15 had managed to find three archers each. Forty-one men just offered their own service as archers.

In fact, the receiver-general's account shows that the earl had recruited more men than he had indented for – 242 as opposed to the promised 200. The costs of over-recruitment had to be met from the earl's own pocket, but it reveals that men were keen to serve and were perhaps hoping for vacancies to arise. Several of the earl's men were already in his service. Nicholas Ledwych, who served as a man-at-arms and had brought three archers, was the earl's steward, while Richard Dull, with two archers, was the master of his horses. Richard Fynch, who served as an archer, was the earl's baker; John Pyntre, archer, was keeper of the earl's robes; and Thomas Norreys, also an archer, was one of the earl's minstrels. At the heart of the earl's retinue was his household, men used to working together who were now called upon to fight together in the service of their master and the king.

# FUNDING THE EXPEDITION

It was at the parliament held at Westminster between 19 November and 7 December 1414 that plans to invade France were first made public. Why did Henry V need to call a parliament in order to go to war? Although kings of England had absolute control over foreign policy, they needed to have the assent of the Commons for taxation: this dated back to the late thirteenth century. On this occasion, the Commons agreed to a double lay subsidy to be collected in two instalments (2 February 1415 and 2 February 1416). On the back of this guaranteed income, the king could start to raise loans. This put Henry in a strong position but it did not give him the ready cash he needed to take an army to France. Troops needed to be paid in advance. Since an embassy sent to France in early 1415 was ineffective, it was clear by March 1415 that Henry would launch an invasion. What he needed the most was cash. To that end, and following customary practice, he sought loans on the security of the tax grants.

The City of London had already shown itself in the past to be a useful provider of loans. However, persuasion was needed. Therefore, on 10 March 1415, Henry summoned the mayor and aldermen and some of the more substantial citizens of London to the Tower of London to tell them that he intended to reconquer the possessions of the Crown in France and that he needed money. This meeting was followed by another one four days later, when the Archbishop of Canterbury, the Bishop of Winchester and the king's youngest brothers, John Duke of Bedford and Humphrey Duke of Gloucester, and the king's cousin, the Duke of York, met the city dignitaries in the Guildhall. A question arose over the order of precedence: the lords agreed that the mayor, as the king's representative in the city, should sit in the middle (i.e. in the place of the greatest honour), with the archbishop and the bishop on his right hand and the dukes to his left. This flattery produced the desired effect. By 16 June, the city had offered the king a loan of 10,000 marks (£6,666 13s 4d – worth almost £2,760,000 today).

As security for the loan, Richard Courtenay, Bishop of Norwich, treasurer of the royal chamber and keeper of the king's jewels (and one of Henry V's closest friends), handed over to the mayor and commonalty as security for the loan a large collar of gold weighing 56 ounces (1.5 kg).

## SUPPLYING THE EXPEDITION

Henry V needed to assemble a large army and fleet for his invasion of France in 1415. However, feeding the thousands of soldiers and sailors for the expedition was a major undertaking. The south coast of England, particularly Southampton and the surrounding region, was the mustering point for the English army. This is likely to have placed enormous demands on the resources of the area to provide for thousands of soldiers, but royal records give us important insights into how food supplies were ensured. On 27 May 1415, the king ordered a proclamation to be made in the town of Southampton and city of Winchester for bread to be baked in anticipation of the arrival of the army. In late June, sheriffs in the counties of south-east England, including Hampshire, were ordered to provide live animals for the expedition. They were collected at Titchfield, Southwick, Beaulieu, Lymington, Romsey, Alresford, Fareham and Southampton, where they were sold to the captains: each captain was responsible for feeding his retinue.

A week before the expedition sailed, on 24 July, the sheriff of Hampshire was ordered to proclaim that all participants in the expedition should each take with them enough supplies to last for at least three months. The need to obtain sufficient quantities of food and drink is likely to have caused problems with the local inhabitants. The royal order of 24 July invited anyone who had suffered molestation from soldiers to lodge their complaints before the steward and controller of the household. Four days later, the king heard that English and Welsh soldiers passing through Warminster had taken goods without paying. The king, concerned at the bad example this might set, commanded that they pay for the goods. If they did not, then the Sheriff of Wiltshire could call out his posse to force the soldiers to make payment.

 # THE CITY OF SALISBURY

In the fifteenth century, Salisbury was a wealthy and populous city due to its manufacture of cloth. In the late fourteenth century, its population may have been as high as 4,800 people. The king's expedition to France was a costly undertaking. Taxation granted by the Commons at the parliament of November 1414 required a levy of a tenth on the value of moveable goods in towns and a fifteenth in the countryside by 2 February 1415, with another payment of the same level a year later.

We see in the Salisbury city records how the royal order for the collection of this tax was exhibited at the city assembly on 11 January 1415. The assembly elected assessors and commissioners to collect the tax in the city. However, the financial contribution of Salisbury did not end there. Wealthy places like Salisbury were asked to contribute loans, just as the city of London had been. On 25 February 1415, the assembly met to discuss the arrival of the Duke of York and Henry Beaufort, Bishop of Winchester (who was also Chancellor of England), who came with a letter from the king requesting a loan. This letter was exhibited to the citizens on 2 March. After a discussion with the duke and bishop, it was decided to advance a loan of £100, which was raised from 86 inhabitants of the city.

The assembly again met on 11 April and decided to appoint Walter Shirle to travel to the king himself to seek sureties for the repayment of the loan. However, Walter reported back to the city on 17 June that he could not obtain a surety of the loan until the arrival of the king in "these parts". (Henry left London to move towards the south coast on 16 June.) The money was therefore entrusted to Shirle's safekeeping until they could decide how to proceed. It appears that Walter was soon pressured into handing the money over to the king. On 3 July, having come from the king's council at Winchester, he informed the assembly that had he not paid the money to the king, the community would have incurred the king's anger. But he had been able to receive an assurance that the loan would be repaid from the customs of Southampton at a later date. The citizens were evidently not displeased with Walter Shirle as he was chosen to be one of two MPs for the city in the parliament of the same year (November 1415). The crown repaid the city's loan in January 1418.

 ## MUSTERING THE ARMY

Having a large number of troops in a concentrated area was potentially disruptive for the local population, both in terms of victualling and military discipline. In addition to the soldiers who had taken goods at Warminster without paying for them, troops from Lancashire, lodging at Fisherton, had attacked the men of the nearby city of Salisbury, driving them off with arrows and swords (this seems to have been a group of Lancashire archers under the command of their knights and esquires). Four of the citizens of Salisbury were killed. The city council debated what to do about this disaster, and had the bells of the city churches sounded as a signal of the possible danger as the troops moved on. Money was spent on additional watches "against hostile strangers". One of those killed was buried at the city's expense.

As we can see from the muster rolls, the various companies of troops arriving for the expedition were ordered to gather in different locations, no doubt reflecting the view that it was better to keep the soldiers dispersed rather than concentrated. The Duke of Gloucester's 800 men were mustered at Michelmersh near Romsey, the Earl of Oxford's 100 men in Over and Middle Wallop. The 960 men under the Duke of Clarence were mustered at "St Catherine's Hill near the New Forest", which suggests a location near Christchurch. The Earl of Huntingdon's 60-strong force was ordered to gather at Swanwick Heath along with the similarly sized companies of Lord Botreaux and Sir John Grey of Ruthin, the 48 men under Sir Roland Lenthale and most of the royal household contingent, which numbered several hundred. Others from the royal household and retinues of the king's knights and esquires were mustered on Hampton Hill. Sir Thomas Erpingham, with 80 men, Sir John Robessart with 24 men, and various other companies mustered on Southampton Heath (now Common).

 ## THE KING'S SHIPS

In late medieval England, royal ships were the personal property of the king and ship numbers fluctuated markedly over time. A royal navy did not exist as such and vessels were often disposed of to pay debts, as occurred after the death of Edward III in 1377. Henry V inherited eight ships on his accession to the throne, which had doubled to 16 by 1416. The largest royal ship in 1415 was the *Trinity Royal* of 540 tons. This was a clinker-built (constructed with overlapping planks), two-masted vessel, which had been rebuilt in 1413 and served as the flagship on the Agincourt expedition. These ships were equipped with a variety of weapons, with the *Thomas of the Tower* of 180 tons, armed with four guns, 20 lances, 15 bows and 11 dozen darts.

The royal vessels, while not in active service, were moored in the Thames near to the Tower of London. Construction and repair work was carried out further down the river at Greenwich, where the ships could be beached in the winter. Henry V's need to build up a large fleet for his war with France meant that shipbuilding was also carried out at other locations, such as Southampton and Winchelsea. These ships only comprised a small proportion of the vessels used in naval expeditions, however, as the vast majority of ships used were hired or impressed merchant ships. In 1415, Henry V hired ships from the Low Countries. Nevertheless, royal ships served an important role as warships, troop transports and for diplomatic missions.

 SOUTHAMPTON AND SHIPPING

In the summer of 1415, all ships over 20 tons at London were ordered to assemble at Southampton to transport Henry V's army to France. Southampton had also been chosen by Henry as a location where some of his ships would be constructed. These works were carried out by William Soper, a wealthy burgess of the town (who later served as an MP and had an affair with the niece of his fellow MP!).

In late February 1414, Soper received £300 in part payment for rebuilding a large Spanish ship called the *Saint Claire of Ipsam*, as the *Holy Ghost of the Tower*. In the summer of 1414, he received a further £496 4s 2d towards the construction of the vessel and £20 for its cables. A further £125 was given to Soper for this purpose in October, together with £20 for cables purchased from a roper of Bridport. In January 1415, further work was carried out on the ship. This included the painting of swans, antelopes and coats of arms on the ship. A later inventory of 1416 for the *Holy Ghost* showed that its armament included seven guns, 14 bows, 91 sheaves of arrows, six crossbows, three pole-axes and 27 bascinets (helmets).

Southampton had been one of the first places to see military action in the Hundred Years War. In the aftermath of a devastating French raid in 1338, the townspeople had spent considerable sums of money on building a complete circuit of stone walls. These works continued into the reign of Henry V. By 1417, God's House Tower had been constructed at the south-east corner of the town. This was one of the earliest types of fortification constructed in England that was designed specifically for the use of gunpowder weapons (see Chapter 13).

# 4

# SOLDIERS

 PEERS

In late medieval England, hereditary noble status was limited to those who received a personal summons to parliament. At any one time, there were between 45 and 60 "parliamentary peers", made up of a small number of dukes (almost exclusively members of the royal family) and a slightly larger number of earls, with the majority being barons (who bore the title "lord"). New titles of marquis and viscount were also seen occasionally. Men might be promoted because of their military prowess and their value as commanders: John, Lord Talbot, for instance, was created Earl of Shrewsbury in 1442 for his service in France. Such promotion was both a reward and an incentive to continue in royal military service. Talbot was prominent in the campaigns of the 1440s and early 1450s. He died at the Battle of Castillon in 1453 leading the last English effort to keep hold of Gascony.

Of the 269 men who held peerage titles between the reopening of the Hundred Years War in 1369 and the loss of Gascony in 1453, at least 247 (92 per cent) can be shown to have been involved in military service to the Crown at least once, either before or after they succeeded to their title. The upbringing of a nobleman, even from an early age, focused on martial arts, especially the handling of weapons and horses. At least two-thirds of the sample was involved in paid military service to the Crown between the ages of 16 and 25. Some were blooded even younger: Henry, Earl of Somerset, was only 14 when he served within the retinue of his step-father, Thomas, Duke of Clarence, on the 1415 expedition, but was not present at Agincourt as he was invalided home from the siege of Harfleur. Alongside him had been Humphrey, Lord FitzWalter, aged 16, who died at the siege on 1 September. Military action could be dangerous: although Thomas Montague, Earl of Salisbury, survived Agincourt and led the invasion into Maine in the mid-1420s, he died on 3 November 1428 from a cannon ball which hit his face during the siege of Orléans. None the less, we see that many peers continued in action into their fifties and sixties. Thomas, Lord Camoys, commander of the rearguard at Agincourt, was 65 at the time of the battle. Peers often had very lengthy military careers.

If the king was not campaigning in person, peers were entrusted with the command of expeditions. The 1412 campaign to France was led by Thomas, Duke of Clarence. Where the king was leading an expedition himself, peers were expected to accompany him. The campaign of 1415 saw 28 in service, although only 17 were present at the battle. In addition to those who died at the siege or were invalided home, some were placed into the garrison of Harfleur: the king's half-uncle Thomas Beaufort, Earl of Dorset, was appointed its captain and appears to have had four barons serving alongside him, at least by the end of the year. Peers also brought the largest retinues since their local and national power enabled them to recruit men more easily. Besides, raising a large company was in itself a mark of esteem and of military reputation. The 28 peers who entered into indentures for the campaign (the two under-age peers, Somerset and FitzWalter did not do so) provided 5,222 men in total. The king relied on his peers for military advice as well as for political support.

# KNIGHTS

The military nature of knighthood is often emphasized but, in reality, the number of knights was declining in the late fourteenth and fifteenth centuries in England. This decline has not been satisfactorily explained. Knighthood in England was not hereditary and knights had to be created. It appears that the Crown was becoming more selective in choosing those to dub as knights. Also it was discovering, especially in military contexts, that it could rely on those of the rank of esquire for professional service and leadership. This had a financial benefit. Esquires were paid one shilling a day by the Crown for their military service, whereas a knight bachelor was paid two shillings. The higher rank of knight, the knight banneret, received four shillings, the same level as a baron. A particularly notable decrease can be seen in the number of knights banneret from the late fourteenth century onwards. Although some men of this status, such as Sir Thomas Erpingham, were present on the campaign, the majority of knights present were knights bachelor. Taking the two groups together, we find 58 knights present. Some indented directly with the Crown, providing over 2,500 soldiers in all, but other knights served in the retinues of peers, providing their companies as part of the overall troop for which the peer had indented. This also suggests that knights acted as sub-commanders.

Campaigns were traditionally contexts in which new knights could be created, especially if an esquire had performed an act of particular valour or tactical significance. We know that some men were dubbed at the initial landing. These included Thomas Geney and John Calthorpe within the retinue of Sir Thomas Erpingham. According to the chronicle of Peter Basset, several were dubbed at Pont-Saint-Maxence during the march eastwards along the Somme.

What is not well-documented, however, is the creation of knights on the eve or morning of the Battle of Agincourt, although such a context was a common time for new knights to be made or promoted. For example, William Oldhall, who served as a man-at-arms in 1415, was knighted before the Battle of Cravant in 1423. Sir John Fastolf, who was present as an esquire on the 1415 campaign (although invalided home), was knighted by 29 January 1416, presumably for his role in the defence of Harfleur, being also granted the lordship of Frileuse close to the captured town. (At Harfleur, in the early months of 1416 we find 22 knights serving in the garrison.) Fastolf was promoted to knight banneret before the Battle of Verneuil in August 1424. There are a number of men known to be esquires when the campaign of 1415 began who appear in 1416 as knights. Therefore, it is very likely that Henry V did dub men knights before the battle. The chronicle written by a priest with Henry's army, the *Gesta Henrici Quinti* (the "Deeds of Henry V"), includes in the list of English casualties "two newly dubbed knights who had fallen in the line of battle". Tradition has it that one of these was Davy Gam of Brecon but this is difficult to prove.

 MEN-AT-ARMS

In military terms, the peers and knights served as men-at-arms, but there were many others without titles who also served in this military capacity. In the late fourteenth and early fifteenth centuries, the term "esquire" was used for these "ordinary" (i.e. non-titled) men-at-arms. This is indicated by the use of the term in the muster lists. These were men who had trained in military activity from an early age, and had the resources and equipment to follow a military career. Their social status in the middling and lower gentry derived from these characteristics. Several indented directly with the Crown for the 1415 expedition, providing at least 1,300 men in total.

As the fifteenth century progressed, however, the use of the term esquire, like that of knight, became more exclusive and limited only to the senior men-at-arms in a retinue. The proportion of men-at-arms to archers also changed. In the late fourteenth century, expeditionary armies tended to have one man-at-arms for every archer. By 1415, the ratio was 1:3, but by the 1430s it was rising to 1:5 and had reached as high as 1:9 by the time of the loss of Normandy in 1449. By 1415, too, the term "lance" was being used for the ordinary men-at-arms. This was based on the common equipment of the rank. These were men who had a complete "harness" (the term for what we now call a suit of armour) made of steel plate. In a battle, they would be expected to play a full role in the melee. They were paid 12d (one shilling) per day.

Men-at-arms also had a right to a share of a bonus paid to captains, known as the "regard". This bonus had been introduced in the 1370s to replace the previous system of evaluation of horses. It was paid at the rate of 100 marks (£66 13s 4d) per 30 men-at-arms for every three-month period in service. This seems an odd amount to us but was obviously easier to administer than the actual appraisal of each horse that a man had with him. We also know that men-at-arms might have a page accompanying them (knights and peers would have had more servants with them, although some served within their retinues as men-at-arms and archers).

 ## ARCHERS

Archers were the most common soldiers found in late medieval English armies, taking both definitions of the word. They were the most numerous but also the least socially elevated. That is not to say they came from the lowest rungs of the social ladder but that they came from the upper peasantry and servants of the households of nobles, knights and esquires. Some were younger members of the families of esquires, who served as archers at the beginning of their careers before becoming men-at-arms as they reached their late teens or early twenties. Indeed, it is significant that in the late fourteenth and early fifteenth centuries they are often listed in muster rolls under the heading "yeoman" (*valettus* in Latin, *valet* in French). This word indicated a strong "service" role, both militarily and domestically. As the fifteenth century progressed, the term yeoman was applied more broadly in society as a whole, indicating the wealthier ranks of the peasantry, and its use as a term for archer declined, although it never fully disappeared.

The English Crown had raised large numbers of archers in the past, perhaps as many as 26,000 in Edward I's Scottish wars of 1298. In the first decade of the fifteenth century, the English Crown came to prefer a ratio of three archers to every one man-at-arms as the optimum. Already by this point, archers were normally expected to be mounted and were paid 6d per day. That is not to say that they fought on horseback but that they had a horse that enabled them to move at the same pace as the rest of the army. They were undoubtedly easier to recruit than men-at-arms because there was a bigger pool to draw from. All adult males were expected to train at the butts on Sundays. English archers were noted overseas for their skill with the bow. The Italian chronicler Giovanni Villani, writing in the 1360s, spoke of how expert and dextrous they were.

In addition to their bow, archers were expected to have a sword and dagger and some kind of body protection and helmet, but they would not have worn full plate armour. Some archers are known also to have been as adept in the use of the crossbow. We know that in the garrisons that the English maintained in Normandy in the 1420s to 1440s, archers might have an additional function, as, for instance, a barber, bowyer or carpenter. Military service as an archer was a good career: a year's service on a campaign or in garrison netted more than a skilled craftsman could earn.

We find some archers with long careers: a few in the garrison of Harfleur under English rule served for 20 years. William Bowyer, who was there in the early months of 1416 and may even have joined the garrison when it was first established, was still there in 1434 (his surname possibly indicating he had a role in the production of the weapon too). Hegyn (or Hugh) Tomson was also there in 1416 and was still there in 1445, presumably finding another posting in the years Harfleur was in French hands in the late 1430s. Some career archers in Harfleur also took advantage of the English policy to grant houses to soldiers. Tomson was one of them, being granted a house near the church of St Martin, as well as another ruined house with its garden, in February 1420.

Furthermore, there was the prospect of gains of war. Some prisoners at Agincourt are known to have been captured by archers who thereby shared in the ransoms. However, the hierarchical nature of the army is reflected in the fact that men-at-arms and captains were also entitled to a share of the gains of their archers, just as the Crown was entitled to a share of everyone's war profits since the Crown had financed the expedition in the first place.

 WELSH ARCHERS

Despite popular tradition, Welsh archers were in a minority in the 1415 army. A few served in the retinues of the peers, knights and esquires, but the main group were the 500 recruited in South Wales. These were drawn from the southern shires of the principality of Wales, Cardiganshire and Carmarthenshire, as well as from the Lancastrian lordship of Kidwelly and the Bohun lordships of Brecon and Hay, which had come to Henry IV (Bolingbroke) through his marriage to Mary de Bohun. These troops were organized by John Merbury, Chamberlain of south Wales. The archers were led by men-at-arms, who received pay at Brecon on 26 June for their companies. The Brecon and Hay contingent was headed by 10 men-at-arms, paid the customary shilling per day for that rank. It contained 14 mounted archers paid 6d per day and 146 foot archers paid 4d per day. The Kidwelly company was made up of three of each category of soldier. The shires of the principality were headed by 10 men-at-arms leading 13 mounted archers and 323 foot archers.

Henry V was keen to take as large an army as possible to France in 1415. Therefore he exploited his close links through the duchy of Lancaster with the county of Lancashire, from which 500 archers were also raised, divided into companies of 50 each under a man-at-arms or knight. The king's position as direct ruler of the county palatine of Chester led to an intention to recruit 650 from there, although it is uncertain whether this number was achieved. There were earlier campaigns in which special archer companies from Wales, Lancashire and Cheshire had been recruited – in 1400, for example, Henry IV had raised 488 archers in Cheshire with 56 men-at-arms – but 1415 appears to be the first and last time that all three areas were called upon at the same time to provide troops. There was no effort to recruit archers in North Wales, however, since there were still suspicions of loyalty in the wake of the revolt of Owain Glyndŵr. Indeed, Owain had never been captured – before the expedition set out, Henry had men sent into North Wales to try to find him to negotiate an amnesty so that the king could be assured there would be no trouble in his absence overseas. However, the erstwhile rebel could not be found and it is generally considered that he died in the same year.

# GUNNERS

Gunners are first recorded in English service in 1346, during the reign of Edward III. This coincides with the earliest use of guns by the English at the Battle of Crécy (26 August 1346) and the siege of Calais (4 September 1346 to 3 August 1347). However these professionals were only employed in small numbers prior to the reign of Henry V. Twenty-six master gunners were recruited for the 1415 expedition in addition to a further 52 assistant gunners. The majority of these men were of Dutch or German origin judging from their names, such as William Gerardson and

Godfrey Goykyn. They are likely to have been recruited by the knight William Van Isendorne, who was paid by the Exchequer on 23 October 1414 for procuring the services of master gunners and gunpowder. Henry V was following past practice in this regard by employing foreign gunners who had been present in the Calais garrison since the fourteenth century. What was unusual about the 1415 expedition was the large numbers employed. The main role of the gunners during the campaign was to maintain the king's guns and to oversee their operation during the siege of Harfleur. In this task, they were assisted by labourers who carried out much of the hard physical work, such as the moving and loading of the guns. Many of the gunners subsequently served as part of the garrison of Harfleur after its capture.

These gunners were skilled professionals who were paid to perform a variety of different tasks. Some idea of the skills necessary to be a gunner can be seen from surviving copies of the *Feuerwerkbuch* (The Firework Book). This was a manual written in German for gunners, written around 1400, which gave advice on different matters including how to mix gunpowder using the components of saltpetre, sulphur and charcoal. Gunners were also often paid to construct wrought iron guns, which would have been forged using smithy skills. The skills of continental gunners continued to be prized by English monarchs throughout the fifteenth and sixteenth centuries. The standard rate of pay for a master gunner in the fifteenth century was 12d (one shilling) whereas assistant gunners were often paid 6d per day. A master gunner therefore received as much as a man-at-arms, and an assistant the same wage as an archer. Assistants were often called "valet gunners", echoing the terminology used for archers.

# 5

# THE SIEGE OF HARFLEUR

 THE LANDING

Making a landing with a large army, its horses and equipment was a major military undertaking in its own right. Henry's fleet dropped anchor at around 5.00 pm on 13 August in the Seine estuary, close by modern Le Havre. The landing area (probably at St Adresse) was described as very stony with large boulders that were dangerous for ships. Behind the shore were deep, water-filled ditches, and beyond these thick earth walls with ramparts. To the east of the landing beaches, the ground rose steeply and the castle of Vitanval stood on the high ground where a later fifteenth century manor house now stands. The low ground on the north bank of the Seine was marshy and reported as having been difficult to cross. Thus, the area was readily defensible, and yet there were no French troops to hinder the landing. The French had found it difficult to anticipate where Henry would land.

Although the king ordered that no one was to land before he had done so – to ensure that the landing was controlled and that troops did not disperse in search of plunder – he sent scouts ashore early on the morning of 14 August to confirm that the area immediately inland from the landing beaches was clear of enemy forces. The main disembarkation began in the afternoon. Rather than attempting to cross the marshes, the army climbed on to the higher ground. Moving the heavy equipment and cannon off the beaches and onto the ridge would have been a laborious and time-consuming process; the disembarkation was not completed until three days later on 17 August.

The high ground to the north of the Seine extends to the east for about six miles (10 km) from the coast, and then falls rapidly to the valley of the river Lézarde and the town of Harfleur. In 1415, this sprawling urban area was largely cultivated land, hamlets and orchards. There was scrub woodland on the slopes towards the Seine. Henry is said to have spent his first night ashore at the priory of Graville, 1.5 miles (2.5 km) west of Harfleur, but as the landings progressed Henry set up his siege camp at Mont Lecomte with a commanding view down into the town of Harfleur to the south-east. On the night of 18 August, the Duke of Clarence was sent to the east of Harfleur with the vanguard. He set up his camp to the north of the town on Mont Cabert, also with a commanding view of the town.

 THE BEGINNING OF THE SIEGE

The river Lézarde runs south through Harfleur into the Seine. To the west, east and north of Harfleur, there was high ground, but to the south of the town, towards the Seine, the ground was low lying. It has long since been drained and developed, but in 1415 it was marshland. When news of the English landings reached the town, the townspeople closed sluice gates to cause the Lézarde to burst its banks and flood the area to the west and north-west of the town, between the walls and the high ground. By the time Henry's men reached Harfleur, the water was already thigh deep. As a consequence, Clarence's deployment to the east of the town required his men to skirt round well to the north, covering a distance of about 10 miles (16 km).

The town of Harfleur, with a population perhaps as high as 5,000, was defended by walls 9,500 feet (2,900 m) long with 22 interval towers, water-filled ditches perhaps 15 feet (4.5 m) deep with steep banks, and three gates. All of these gates were well protected by outworks constructed of tree trunks lashed together and driven into the ground, with earth and further wood inside to add strength. The outworks were pierced with embrasures for small guns and crossbows. The town gates were protected by drawbridges and flanked by towers. These defences were further enhanced by a fortified port to the south of the town. The entrance to the port was defended with chains drawn across the entrance channel between two towers. The town had prepared for a possible attack by stocking up timber and stone. The inhabitants even tore up paving slabs from the causeway leading north towards Montivilliers to supplement their materials for maintaining the defences.

The defence of Harfleur was in the hands of Louis, Sire d'Estouteville, and Raoul de Gaucourt. They had at their disposal a militia drawn from the population and there were also some cross-bowmen and men-at-arms. Reinforcements arrived on 18 August before Clarence could establish his position on Mont Cabert, bringing the total number of knights and men-at-arms to about 260. The defenders were also equipped with artillery and had stocks of catapults and large crossbows.

Henry started his investment of Harfleur on 17 August. By 23 August, the siege was sufficiently well established for the inhabitants to send word to Charles d'Albret, the Constable of France, in Rouen, that they could no longer make contact by land.

 # BOMBARDMENT

Henry had come to France fully prepared for a siege campaign against Harfleur and other places in Normandy. He had brought siege engines, cannon and professional gunners, including 30

or so recruited from outside England. Hoardings were made to shelter the guns and gunners. These were lifted when the guns were to be fired. Buildings outside the walls were demolished by the English to allow for artillery to be used to best effect. During the siege, Henry's attempts to wear down the defences with guns and throwing machines had some success. However, at night, the French carried out repairs using timber and tubs filled with earth, dung, sand and stones, and walls were shored up with faggots, earth and clay. They covered their streets with sand to prevent stone cannon balls splintering on impact. These efforts could do no more than delay the destruction of the defences, however, and eventually the outer barbicans were abandoned with guns being repositioned inside.

Over the duration of the siege, the bombardment caused considerable damage both to the town defences and houses – the repairs to the fortifications took a number of years, and the poor state of buildings within the town proved to be a strong disincentive when Henry was seeking to encourage English people to settle there. It is indicative of the destruction that, although there are a number of domestic buildings in the town surviving from the fifteenth century, their construction is generally attributed to the latter part of the century.

 MINING

While the bombardment of Harfleur was underway there were also attempts to undermine the defences. The objective was to tunnel under weak points in the walls or a tower. Tunnels would be shored up with timber props and at the chosen moment the props would be set alight to induce the collapse of the tunnel and bring down whatever was above it. During the siege of Harfleur, mining was undertaken by Clarence's men on the eastern side of the town where the conditions were better. The French undertook counter mining to either destroy or break into the English mines. Where the mines could be penetrated, there was underground fighting to disrupt work. The situation in Harfleur prevented the English from starting their work out of sight and even the construction of a shelter did not fool the French. French countermeasures thwarted three attempts to mine the defences. The mines were abandoned and subsequently filled in during the English occupation, which, although the town was once again in French hands between 1435 and 1445, did not finally end until 1450.

 DISEASE

Medieval besiegers were often as badly placed as the besieged, and disease in insanitary camps was always a hazard. At Harfleur, the poor sanitary conditions to which Henry's men were exposed were exacerbated by unseasonably warm weather, polluted water, difficulties in disposing of carcasses and other rubbish and the generally humid conditions. At some point during the siege, the English had managed to cut off the flow of water from the Lézarde to the north of Harfleur. As a result, the floodwaters had subsided, but the result would have been stagnant, marshy water that compounded the humid conditions.

The result of the poor sanitation and the weather was dysentery. The disease did not prejudice the success of the siege, but it had a serious impact on some parts of the army, leading to the death, among others, of Richard Courtenay, Bishop of Norwich and Michael de la Pole, Earl of Suffolk. The number of troops who died during the siege due to dysentery was small. However, the impact stretched beyond the fatalities since at least 1,300 combatants had to be invalided home to England.

 ASSAULT

Early in the siege, Henry offered terms to Harfleur. A chaplain with the army, who wrote a narrative of the campaign in *Gesta Henrici Quinti*, remarked that these were in accordance with the Book of Deuteronomy: either peace in return for surrender or, if the town had to be taken by assault, no quarter for the male inhabitants with women and property liable to be carried off as spoils of war.

The prospect of an English assault hung over the population throughout the siege. However, for most of the siege the English contented themselves with tightening the blockade and maintaining a near-continuous bombardment, supplemented by attempts to bring down defences through mining. It was not until 16 September that the first serious assault was made. Ironically, this was provoked by a sally out of the Leure gate by the French the night before, which had resulted in some of the English siege works being set alight. The English filled the ditch around the bastion protecting the gate, and drove the defenders back within the main town walls.

The following night, overt English preparations for a final assault were sufficient to convince the inhabitants of the town that it would be wise to surrender. Trumpeters had been sent around the siege camps to proclaim that there would be an assault the next morning and that every sailor and soldier should prepare themselves. Orders were also given to intensify the bombardment throughout the night with the objectives of hampering repairs and to keep the defenders from sleeping. At dawn on 18 September, before the assault began, an offer for a conditional surrender was made by the town council.

# THE FRENCH RESPONSE

The French had taken some preliminary measures to counter the anticipated English landing. Even as early as June, the French nobility had been given notice to prepare themselves. Shortly after the start of the siege, Charles d'Albret, Constable of France, sent word to the king and the dauphin in Paris of the arrival of Henry. The constable also responded to a request from the inhabitants when the encirclement by land was complete, for a boat to be provided to help with the provisioning of the town and to enable messages to be passed between the besieged town and himself. Albret arranged for a small galley, which had the advantage of being powered by oars, to be sent down the Seine from Rouen.

On 28 August, the nobility in Normandy and surrounding areas was called to arms, with Rouen to be nominated as the point of rendezvous. The dauphin was to go to Normandy as the king's lieutenant and captain general as the French army began to gather. The king indicated his intention to follow soon to raise the siege. On 10 September, he attended mass in the abbey of St-Denis north of Paris. The *Oriflamme*, the royal banner held in the abbey and used in battles where the king was present in person to signify that no quarter would be given, was entrusted to Guillaume VIII Martel, the Sire de Bacqueville, whose lordship lay in the pays de Caux north of Harfleur.

In early September, news reached the dauphin that Harfleur was in desperate need of reinforcement. By 13 September, he had reached Vernon on the river Seine, and here he received further envoys carrying news of the plight of Harfleur. Henry had an effective blockade in place by land and by sea, with ships on the Seine and smaller boats in the area flooded by the Lézarde. Between 14 and 16 September, the constable attempted, but failed, to break the stranglehold of the cordon around the town by sending a small fleet from Rouen. The attempt to relieve Harfleur failed and hope for the town was running out.

Harfleur's envoys to the dauphin had been assured that the king was gathering his army and would come to their aid. This was partially true, but when the dauphin was reassuring the envoys, there were no more than a few thousand troops available. Furthermore, these were dispersed across several locations to enable the French to respond to possible English movements. The French were in no position to relieve the siege.

 ## THE SURRENDER OF THE TOWN

After the townspeople asked for terms on 18 September, the king sent in Thomas Beaufort, Earl of Dorset, Henry, Lord Fitzhugh, and Sir Thomas Erpingham to negotiate terms. Henry had wanted the surrender to be made the following day, but conceded that more time could be given to the inhabitants. It was agreed that the town would be surrendered if neither the king nor the dauphin had come to its relief by 1.00 pm on Sunday 22 September.

The Sire de Hacqueville set out to notify the dauphin and ask for urgent assistance. When he arrived at Vernon, the dauphin broke the news that the assembly of the army was not complete and that assistance would not be forthcoming. However, given that Hacqueville probably took two days to reach the dauphin at Vernon, even if the French army had assembled, relief of the town before 22 September would not have been possible.

Henry took the formal surrender in person on 22 September in his pavilion on Mont Lecomte. The next day, he entered Harfleur. Dismounting on entering the town, Henry gave thanks in the Church of St Martin and emphasized his belief that his victory was God-given. The French captains were free to go, subject to agreeing under oath to report to Calais on 11 November. Civilians were separated into two groups: those swearing fealty to Henry and those being retained in custody against payment of ransoms. Women, children, the poor and the helpless – numbering between 1,500 and 2,000 – were expelled from the town on 24 September, in part because the town was in no condition to support the population. They took with them their clothing, all that they could carry and five sous. They were escorted by the English to Lillebonne, 20 miles (32 km) to the east, where they were handed over to Marshal Boucicaut who gave them food and water.

Henry took steps to establish Harfleur as an English colony on a similar basis to Calais. He garrisoned the town with 300 men-at-arms and 900 archers, appointing the Earl of Dorset as captain. His plan was to encourage settlement. On 5 October, the sheriffs of London were ordered to proclaim that all merchants, victuallers and artificers who were willing to reside in Harfleur should go to the town with all speed where they would be given houses. Henry had the municipal records and existing title deeds burned in the market place: henceforward, the purchase and inheritance of land were to be restricted to Englishmen, with French inhabitants being reduced to the status of lessees. Orders were given for the repair of the town and for its provisioning from England.

# 6

# THE MARCH

 LEAVING HARFLEUR

Once Henry had taken the surrender of Harfleur on 22 September 1415, he wrote to the city of London announcing his success. Four days later, he sent Raoul de Gaucourt to the dauphin with a challenge for personal combat. Henry's proposal was that the outcome would resolve his claims in France, with the proviso that Charles VI should continue to reign for the rest of his days with the crown passing to Henry on his death. Henry waited at Harfleur for eight days to give the dauphin the chance to respond. The dauphin could neither accept nor refuse the challenge; his only option was to ignore it. Henry could not have expected the dauphin to do otherwise than decline to reply, but he had secured a propaganda victory and given himself some thinking time while the eight days given for a reply elapsed.

Henry decided not to attempt further conquests but chose instead to leave France by marching his army straight to Calais. His decision was based on the fact that his army was diminished in size by at least 25 per cent. There had been some desertions, and some troops had died during the siege, due both to hostile action and dysentery (which had been contracted in the English camps). In addition to the deaths from dysentery, more than 1,300 combatants had to be sent back home. The defences of Harfleur had been so damaged that Henry had needed to install a garrison of 1,200 men, together with the gunners and carpenters, to ensure its defence. The size of the army available to Henry for his onward march was most likely around 8,500, or 500 or so each side of this figure. Of these, in excess of 7,000 were archers. This was still a good-sized army for the period. Indeed, the size of Henry's army had dissuaded the French king and dauphin from moving down the Seine to Rouen. They only began to do so once Henry had left Harfleur, arriving in the Norman capital on 12 October.

Henry began his march northwards on 8 October. Neither his departure nor his direction of travel would have come as a surprise to the French, since news of his intent to march to Calais had reached Boulogne two days before.

 ## THE ROUTE

Henry's intended route was directly towards Calais, 170 miles (270 km) away. It is clear that he hoped to get to Calais as quickly as possible. This suggests that he was not seeking battle with the French. If that had been his objective, then he would surely have headed towards Rouen where, as he must have known, the French army was gathering. A move northwards also had the added advantage of drawing the French away from an early attack on Harfleur. As Henry marched across the pays de Caux, he did not attempt any conquest. His army was still large enough to scare the local population: at both Arques and Eu, the townspeople bought off any damage with offers of food to the English army.

The ford at Blanchetaque, between the estuary of the Somme and Abbeville, was on the direct route from Harfleur to Calais. However, it was an obvious place for Henry's army to attempt to cross the Somme. By the time the English approached the ford, the French were gathered in strength on the far side of the river. In

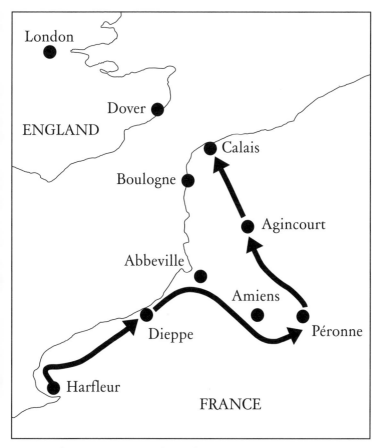

*Route of Henry V's army through France.*

1346, Henry's great-grandfather, Edward III, had forced a crossing of the Somme here. However, with 14,000 men, Edward's army had been much larger than Henry's.

Henry had heard that there were 6,000 French troops arrayed to counter his passage of the ford. Although Henry's army was more numerous than the opposition at this point, it would have been extremely vulnerable during the crossing: moving a large army and its equipment across a wide river would have been as hazardous as making the initial landing in France. It is not surprising, therefore, that Henry turned away from Blanchetaque and headed east upstream on the southern bank of the Somme.

Upstream from Blanchetaque, the course of the river is initially fairly straight, but beyond Amiens, the river follows wide, sweeping curves. By cutting across the cord of these bends, Henry was able to overhaul the French and cross the Somme just to the south of Péronne on 19 October. Once across the river, he turned north-west towards Calais, but on arriving at Maisoncelle on 24 October, he found the French army blocking his route. He had covered 260 miles (420 km) since leaving Harfleur, averaging 14 miles (23 km) per day.

 # BLANCHETAQUE

There are several explanations as to why the ford of Blanchetaque, a corruption of the French for a white stain, was so called. The two reasons most widely quoted are that the name was either derived from the causeway being made of white chalk or because of a white chalk mark on the rising ground to the north of the Somme, used as a reference point to guide those crossing the river. Also, an eighteenth-century map shows the name running down the centre of the river close to the estuary.

The river has changed a great deal over the centuries, with construction of a canal and a railway, and reclamation of land. Consequently, it is difficult to visualize what Henry's army would have faced. However, having descended to the river from the higher ground, the flood plain would have been a little under two miles (just over three km) wide before the ground started to rise again on the far side. Even if not all of this stretch was under water at low tide, there would have been extensive marshland adjacent to the river. Even today, with the water controlled by the modern works, the marshy nature of the area is evident and tracks are built on low, elevated causeways. The medieval causeway is said to have been wide enough for 12 men abreast. It is possible that there was a central causeway constructed of chalk to support wheeled vehicles with a wider area useable by horses and those on foot allowing a crossing at low tide. Although we cannot be sure precisely where the ford of Blanchetaque was located, it was probably between Noyelles-sur-Mer and Saigneville.

 ## CROSSING THE SOMME

Henry crossed the Somme on 19 October, probably somewhere between Béthencourt-sur-Somme and Voyennes, 10.5 miles (17 km) south of Péronne. There were two narrow causeways. They had been broken in the middle of the river, but they had not been staked as they should have been. Therefore, a crossing could be made in single file and men-at-arms and archers were sent across to establish a bridgehead and to protect the crossing of the bulk of the army. The causeways were then repaired, using faggots, straw and planks. Some accounts talk of the English demolishing houses and taking shutters, windows and ladders to bridge the gaps. Others describe Henry commandeering labourers and carpenters to fell trees and construct a bridge.

The crossing was carried out with remarkable discipline. Realizing the importance of avoiding congestion, Henry and his senior commanders took a hands-on approach to managing the operation. They positioned themselves by the two causeways to marshal the crossing of men, horses and vehicles with one causeway used for wagons and the other for troops. Once the archers had crossed first to create a defensive bridgehead, a standard was planted and then the remainder of the vanguard crossed, followed by the centre division and the rear-guard.

Around nightfall on 19 October, Henry's army was safely across the river. The crossing had taken the French by surprise.

Some patrols probed the bridgehead to see if they could drive the English back but they were too late. English mounted troops drove them off and the period of vulnerability passed as Henry's strength on the far bank increased. The problem for the French had been that potential crossing points had become more numerous the further upstream that the English moved. With a long stretch of area to watch, the French had been forced to disperse their troops in small groups. The slow communications of the period and the time required to then reassemble the army meant that they could not marshal sufficient troops in time to oppose Henry's crossing, particularly as he drew ahead of the French with the advantage of the sweep of the river.

 # MILITARY DISCIPLINE

Discipline is an important factor in the success of any army. Good leadership, a sense of loyalty to ones comrades and formal discipline all play their part. By the time of the Battle of Agincourt, Henry's army had been together in France for more than two months and through the leadership of the king, the constable, the marshals and the captains of the retinues, had becomes welded into an effective and disciplined fighting force. However, in addition, Henry placed great importance on the formal discipline and correct conduct of his army. He had issued disciplinary ordinances at the opening of the campaign, based on those that had been issued for Richard II's campaign in Scotland in 1385.

As a result, although the army foraged for food as it advanced, the pillaging, burning and destruction which typically accompanied such activities were less than would have been expected from an English army in the time of Edward III during the previous century. Indeed, it seems that the villagers and townspeople suffered more from the passage of the French than they did from Henry's men.

On the eve of battle, Henry was alive to the risk of a surprise attack during the night, and in order that the normal clamour of camp life should not mask the noise of French movement he gave strict orders for silence throughout the army. This order was to be enforced by harsh penalties: gentlemen would forfeit their horses and equipment, and archers and others of lower rank would have their right ear cut off. It is testament to the discipline of the army that the king's order does not seem to have been disobeyed. Overall, it seems that although there were cases of desertion during the siege of Harfleur, examples of breaches of discipline were rare. The only recorded example of Henry imposing a punishment relates to an incident during the march. A soldier was brought before Henry, charged with having stolen a pyx, containing consecrated bread, from a local church. He was hanged for the offence, since it was against the disciplinary code that Henry had issued at the beginning of the campaign, which banned all acts of sacrilege.

 FEEDING THE ARMY

If Henry had been able to march directly to Calais, his army would have faced a march of perhaps 12 days, although the author of *Gesta Henrici Quinti* rather over optimistically spoke of eight days. In the event, due to the longer route Henry was compelled to take, he took 17 days to arrive at Maisoncelle on the eve of battle, and a total of 22 days to get to Calais. Thus, rations were a problem. One chronicle account speaks of men being forced to eat nuts from the hedgerows.

When Henry V set off from Harfleur, he had an army of between eight and nine thousand men. On top of this, he would probably have had several thousand non-combatants, including pages and support staff. Feeding an army of this size presented a huge task – there would have been a daily demand for 15 tonnes or more of food. The horses presented an even bigger challenge

– there could well have been 20,000, and their daily needs for food and water would have been very considerable. Each horse would have required about 55 lb (25 kg) of fresh grass or 22 lb (10 kg) of dry fodder per day. In view of the quantities needed it would not have been practical to carry dry fodder, so each day some 200 tonnes of dry fodder or several hectares of pasture needed to be found. In addition, each horse would have required around four gallons (18 litres) of water per day.

Henry's army was on the move in October. It could be expected that store houses would be replenished, and raiding villages would provide some of the needs of the army. Towns were also persuaded to give supplies of food in return for their safety from destruction. However, French detachments would certainly have harassed foraging parties and villagers would have done their best to hide animals and supplies. As the march progressed, the army became increasingly short of food.

 # FRENCH RESPONSES AND PLANS

The process of mobilizing the French army was slow. It was only at the end of August that the king's council ordered additional taxes to be raised to cover the costs of 6,000 men-at-arms and 3,000 *gens de trait* (crossbowmen and archers). Despite the continuing mobilization, by the time of the surrender of Harfleur on 22 September, the army was still inadequate to relieve the town. Initially, the rendezvous for the gathering French army was Rouen, but with Henry's intention to march towards Calais, the focus for mobilization shifted to the north and beyond the Somme.

The French were determined to intercept and bring the English to battle before they could reach Calais. Initially they had expected the engagement to be as Henry crossed the Somme near its mouth, but he had chosen not to risk this crossing. The

French, commanded at this point by the highly experienced Marshal Boucicaut and Constable Albret, along with the Comte de Richemont and Duke of Alençon, had shadowed him from the north bank of the Somme, carrying out various sorties. When Henry reached Corbie on 17 October, some prisoners he had taken divulged that the French were planning an attack. As a result, he ordered his archers each to prepare a stake six feet (1.8 metres) long, sharpened at both ends. In the event of the anticipated French cavalry attack, the archers were to drive their stakes in front of them as a protection.

The information that Henry had received may have been the document outlining a French plan of battle that was discovered by Dr Christopher Phillpotts in the British Library in 1984. This plan seems to have been drawn up sometime between 13 and 21 October since it only includes those French commanders known to have been north of the Somme between those dates: it does not include other commanders, such as the dukes of Orléans and Bourbon, who were present at the Battle of Agincourt. In the plan, the French proposed two main battles (the term here meaning fighting divisions): the vanguard under Constable d'Albret and Marshal Boucicaut and a second battle commanded by the Duke of Alençon and the Count of Eu. There were to be two wings of men on foot with crossbowmen and archers placed in front of them. There would be a company of 1,000 cavalry with the task of riding down the English archers – exactly as Henry had heard from the prisoners he had taken. A further company of 200 cavalry would attack the baggage train and the rear of the English. If Henry's army fought in one division then the French planned to combine both their battles.

# SUMMONS TO BATTLE

On 20 October, French heralds were despatched to inform Henry of the intent to bring him to battle before he reached Calais. It is not certain whether this summons came from the king and the dauphin in council in Rouen or, more probably, from a council of senior commanders meeting in Péronne. It is also possible that there was coordination between the two councils. With both the king and the dauphin intending to stay away from the battle and the Duke of Berry being too old to fight, the Duke of Orléans, as the next senior member of the Royal family, was the logical person to issue the summons to Henry to join in battle. However, he was still in Orléans on 17 October, having initially been ordered to stay away to avoid opening old wounds with the Duke of Burgundy and he was not summoned to come north until around 20 October.

The French summons to Henry probably proposed a site for the battle at Aubigny-en-Artois, 25 miles (40 km) east/southeast of Agincourt. The French seem to have believed that Henry had accepted this location, and to have set out for Aubigny from Péronne while Henry was still south of the town. Henry's route from Péronne initially took him towards Aubigny. However, on 22 October he changed direction.

Once the French became aware that Henry was moving away from the planned rendezvous, they had to select another place for the battle: somewhere on Henry's expected route towards Calais. They needed a place not so close as to allow reinforcements to sally forth from English garrisons in the Pale of Calais, but somewhere that would also afford them a suitable field of battle. Having selected the open ground near Agincourt and Ruisseauville, they then needed to communicate the change of rendezvous to the companies of men either already en route to Aubigny or simply heading towards the general area of assembly.

In the event, although sufficient forces had been assembled by 24 October to block Henry's march to Calais, the change of rendezvous delayed the arrival of some companies and there were some notable absentees: the Duke of Brittany, who was still 50 miles (80 km) to the west on the eve of battle and the Duke of Brabant, who only arrived after the start of the battle. In addition, the Duke of Burgundy, who was asked not to join the French army because of his feud with the Duke of Orléans, did not bring his men to join the gathering host.

# 7

# THE BATTLE

 ## ON THE EVE OF BATTLE

On 24 October, Henry's army crossed the river Ternoise close to Blangy and climbed out of the river valley onto the gently undulating land beyond, moving towards the village of Maisoncelle. Ahead they could see the gathering French army converging on Agincourt and Ruisseauville and blocking the way to Calais.

Henry arrayed his army in case the French might seek to fight straightaway that day. However, the French army was still assembling and was not yet ready. Facing the prospect of battle, the English – as was the custom – took confession and Henry addressed his men: encouraging them, he said that he would rather die than be taken by the French with the burden of his ransom falling on the English people. Henry's reported rebuke of Sir Walter Hungerford for wishing that there were 10,000 more archers present is immortalized in Shakespeare's *Henry V*. Although Shakespeare puts Hungerford's words into the mouth of the Earl of Westmorland – who was not actually on the campaign – the exchange has become a central part of the legend of Agincourt.

Henry kept his men in formation until sunset on 24 October,

expecting that the French would go to battle. He then repositioned his men to minimize the risk of being encircled by the French as the armies camped for the night: the English centred on Maisoncelle, and the French to their north around Agincourt and Ruisseauville.

To counter the risk of a surprise attack during the night and in order that the normal clamour of camp life should not mask the noise of French movement, Henry gave strict orders for silence throughout the English army, although trumpets and other instruments were sounded in the night to disconcert the French. Both sides carried out reconnaissance during the night and bows, armour and weapons were prepared for the coming battle. However, those that were able to would have rested and slept as much as possible.

Why did the French not wage war against Henry on 24 October? In the French camp, decisions had to be made over their battle plan. The English army was not going to increase in size and the French had nothing to lose by waiting for companies still to arrive.

## ENGLISH DEPLOYMENT AND ARMY SIZE

Henry's army had been reduced in size over the course of the campaign. Taking into account the garrison placed in Harfleur, the losses at the siege and the men invalided home, as well as a few losses on the march, we can suggest that he had around 8,500 fighting men at the battle. But of these, relatively few were men-at-arms – no more than 1,500 at most. Although grouped into three battles (the vanguard on the right under the Duke of York, the centre under the king and the rearguard on the left under Thomas, Lord Camoys), chronicles suggest these battles were kept close to each other and were not many ranks deep. It is impossible to know exactly who was in which battle from the available sources, but the fact that Michael de la Pole, Earl of Suffolk was killed might suggest that he was also in the vanguard.

We would also expect the royal household troops to serve in the king's central division. A financial record suggests that Henry also used the archers from Lancashire as his bodyguard.

The principal debate on English deployment is the position of the archers, who numbered between 7,000 and 7,500. Most likely, the majority were placed in mass formations of serried ranks on each flank of the English army, but some were placed in contingents between and in front of the three battles of men-at-arms. The archers were all protected against the expected French cavalry charge by stakes. Henry also sent 200 archers to woods near Tramecourt, close to the French rearguard: their role was to fire from the rear and side into the French. The long archer formations on the flanks – which in the view of the chronicle writer known as the Religieux de Saint-Denis gave the impression of encirclement of the French – would expose the advancing French to a lengthy barrage of lateral arrow shot.

Henry followed the military teachings of the time – which were based largely on the fourth-century treatise by Vegetius, *De Re Militari* – by adopting a defensive position, as was appropriate for his smaller army. He protected his archers by stakes and placed his baggage behind his army also as a defence. He sought to force the French into making the main forward advance while he maintained his defensive position.

 FRENCH DEPLOYMENT

A new battle plan had been devised at Rouen around 20 October. At this point it was decided that the king and dauphin should not take the field in person, but that the Duke of Orléans (the nephew of the king) should be there, reversing a previous policy that both he and the Duke of Burgundy should stay away because of their political differences. This plan envisaged three battles and two wings of men-at-arms on foot, plus cavalry intended to break the English archers.

On 25 October, however, the French may only to have been able to draw up two battles (the term used in the period for the main groups into which the army was divided for action), reflecting the failure of all troops to arrive in time. Many, including Orléans, appeared quite late in the day, this situation also contributing to the difficulty the French had in organizing themselves. While the English had been together for 10 weeks, the French arrived in dribs and drabs, and differences of opinion emerged over formation as well as action.

The vanguard at the battle, seemingly around 5,000 strong, included Marshal Boucicaut, Constable Albret and the dukes of Orléans and Bourbon. They were a mixture of veteran commanders and inexperienced, hot-headed, young royals. The French chose to create a very large vanguard of men-at-arms, believing that they could win the battle by overwhelming the English men-at-arms by sheer weight of numbers. As a result, they did not make full use of their own missile men, the crossbowmen and longbowmen. Perhaps they realized that these troops were far too outnumbered by their English counterparts. The cavalry forces on each flank, charged with overriding the English archers, were not as large as intended and therefore failed in their purpose. This left the French men-at-arms at the mercy of the arrow storm. Since the French had planned wisely all along to try to attack the English archers, we must ask why they could not find enough cavalry on the day. Contemporary sources tend to suggest that troops were keen to be in the vanguard because that offered them the greatest chance of honour in fighting against men of equal rank as well as the prospect of valuable prisoners – even Henry himself. But it may also be that men were reluctant to expose their horses to English arrows.

FRENCH ARMY SIZE

While the French certainly outnumbered the English, we can dismiss the high figures reported in chronicles, especially the numbers given in some English texts of 100,000 or more. Such numbers were for effect and do not represent reality. This is a common problem but is not restricted to battles. Figures of 40–60,000 given in chronicles for those involved in the Peasants' Revolt of 1381, for instance, exceed the levels of adult population in the counties involved.

Not until the seventeenth century did the French raise armies of six figures. Even 20,000 is too high for 1415, these numbers not being seen until the end of the fifteenth century. Admittedly, we do not have the same level of survival of financial records for the French army at the battle as we do for the English, but we know that to respond to the English invasion, a tax was levied to pay for 6,000 men-at-arms and 3,000 archers. It is not unreasonable to add in more troops to reach a total of 12,000 or so, since the *semonce des nobles* was also used to call on the service of the nobility and those accustomed to follow arms (although they too would have expected pay for their service). But we need to remember that the army was not drawn from the whole of France. The lists of dead and prisoners indicate an overwhelming predominance of troops from Picardy, Artois and Upper Normandy.

Finally, after disaster struck the vanguard, other troops following behind chose not to engage but instead fled the field. Even an attack by the French second division is uncertain. It is also notable that the English do not appear to have conducted a rout to drive away the French: this suggests that they withdrew of their own volition. The overall size of the French army at Agincourt is therefore less significant than the way in which the battle was fought: not all troops present engaged.

# THE ARROW STORM

The two armies faced each other for some time without any sign of the French making the first move. The French were still hoping that more men would arrive. Henry needed to take the initiative in order to force the enemy into an attack. At around 10.00 am, he decided to move forward and bring his archers within range of the French. The signal for the advance was given by Sir Thomas Erpingham throwing a baton into the air. With a great shout and to the sound of trumpets, the English moved forward into a new position. The main body of archers stopped, replanted their stakes and started shooting on the advancing French.

The French were taken by surprise, anticipating that the initiative for the start of combat rested with them. They responded by moving forward. If the French plan to use 1,000 mounted men to ride down and neutralize the archers had been well executed then the cavalry would have been in contact with the archers before the men on foot closed with the English. However, they had lost the initiative and their charge was disordered. Also, it seems that the French could not find all of the cavalry they needed. Men were keener to join the vanguard in the hope of taking important prisoners. In addition, they may not have wanted to have their horses wounded or killed by arrow shot, as surely would be the case.

The shooting of the archers made horses stumble, fall and wheel about to escape the arrows, hindering those who came after and disrupting the vanguard advancing on foot. Those of the cavalry who made it as far as the archers were confronted by the stakes, which disrupted what was left of the cohesion of the charge and increased the vulnerability of the cavalry to point-blank shooting by the archers.

As the men-at-arms advanced on foot, they faced shooting from the archers to their front and on their flank near Tramecourt. As one contemporary account indicates, the French felt themselves encircled by English archers. The effect of the archery from more than 7,000 archers was very destructive, killing and wounding men, and disrupting their formation as they advanced. This was not an experience for which the French men-at-arms could train. It was made more frightening by its intensity: each archer had at least 24 arrows, making possible a storm of 170,000 flights. The shot was probably in bursts of different lengths, so that the French might be lulled into thinking the arrow storm had ended only to find it had recommenced. This was a terrifying experience against which the French had no answer. All they could do was to try to keep up their advance. Although there were fourteenth-century precedents for this situation, including Crécy and Poitiers, French armies had not experienced English armies in the field for many years, and had not anticipated the overwhelming effect of arrow power from so many archers.

The momentum of the advance was diminished, and the situation for the French deteriorated the closer they came as the English shot at point blank range. The shooting drove the French towards the centre. The effects of the arrow storm, as well as the lie of the land and the woods funnelled them into an ever-narrowing front, compressing the French into an unmanageable mass as they made contact with the English men-at-arms.

 ## THE MELEE

The archers had inflicted heavy losses on the vanguard on foot and the cavalry. They alone could not defeat the French, however, and the two armies now clashed in hand-to-hand combat.

As they had made their advance forwards into a new position in order to provoke the French into attack, the English had moved from firm, unploughed land onto soft, newly sown ground that was sodden because of heavy rain. The advance over this ground had been difficult, but they could now hold their position and wait for the French as they came across muddy ground churned up both by the cavalry charge and the out-of-control horses.

The French made for the standards in the centre of each of the three English divisions, but by the time that they made contact they were close to exhaustion. To add to their problems, they had shortened their lances to make them easier to handle in close combat – the English had not done so, and were able to thrust at the French and inflict wounds, particularly to legs and groins, before they could strike. The French, funnelled together both by the topography and by those on the flanks moving inwards to try to avoid the shooting of the archers, were further hampered by the need to keep their visors closed and their heads down in the face of the shooting of the archers. The sheer weight of numbers also worked to their disadvantage. Men crowded upon those in front, and as troops fell killed or wounded, others stumbled and fell. Men piled upon others, further hampering those who came on behind – these were so closely packed that they had great difficulty closing with the English and even raising their weapons.

The combat was ferocious and Henry was closely involved, protecting the wounded Duke of Gloucester. The Duke of Alençon struck the king a blow to the head with an axe, breaking the crown on Henry's helmet, before he was struck down and killed by Henry's bodyguards.

As the French became increasingly vulnerable, especially as they piled up, Henry's archers were able to join in, using their own weapons and those taken from the fallen to deliver blows with axes, maces, pole-axes, mallets, hammers and stakes. Those of the French who had fallen wounded were also vulnerable to stabbing through gaps between pieces of armour and through visors, and many of them suffered wounds to the neck and head.

The French vanguard had been defeated. The greater part of the French leadership had been killed or captured and a severe blow had been delivered to the morale of the main battle. Thus, although some at least of the main battle engaged the English, others fled along with whatever rearguard remained. The battle was apparently won, and the English could start to assemble prisoners, identify the dead and tend the wounded.

 ## THE MASSACRE OF THE PRISONERS

The most controversial episode in the Battle of Agincourt today is the killing of French prisoners. At the end of the first phase of the battle, perhaps two hours or so after it had started, there was a cessation in the fighting during which the English took a number of prisoners from the piles of wounded and dead French men-at-arms. These would have been men who could, or appeared to be, capable of paying sizeable ransoms in return for their lives. However some of these captives were put to death.

The reason for this, according to the account of *Gesta Henrici Quinti*, was that "a shout went up" among the English that the French were regrouping to launch a fresh assault. This was said to have resulted in the English killing all but their most valuable prisoners to stop them from taking up arms again. Other chronicle writers provide similar explanations. Several English accounts emphasize that the victory had already been achieved, implying that Henry had stood his army down. Therefore, they were both exhausted and no longer in fighting array, and in no position to face a new foe as well as potentially the prisoners who, even though wounded, might seek to attack their captors when they saw potential rescuers close at hand.

Some French accounts even name the French who were proposing the new attack. Clignet de Brabant is often blamed, but this may simply be a political gesture by Burgundian writers against a well-known Armagnac captain. In the reminiscence of Ghillebert de Lannoy, who had been taken prisoner in the first phase, it was the arrival of the Duke of Brabant that explained Henry's order. The duke did indeed arrive late at the battle (perhaps around 1.00 pm as he had to travel at least 30 miles [48 km] between Lens and Agincourt) but he engaged in it and was killed. Other narratives suggest that Henry's order was enough to dissuade the new French force from making any attack at all. Writers Jean Le Fèvre and Jean Waurin include a story that Henry's soldiers were reluctant to kill their prisoners because they did not want to lose valuable ransoms and that the king had to order a group of archers to carry out his order.

Only one account, that of the Artois author Pierre de Fenin, claims that the massacre was a response to a French attack on the English baggage train at the rear of the English lines. Such an attack did occur, with the king even losing some of his possessions. A raid on the baggage had been part of the French battle plan drawn up for an engagement along the Somme, but it is possible that the attackers at Agincourt were local peasants rather than from the French army.

 THE DEAD

We cannot be certain which men died in the battle and which as a result of the killing of the prisoners. Chronicles estimate the numbers of French dead to be anywhere between 3,000 and 12,000, but these figures are as problematic as the numbers given for the French army as a whole. The Burgundian chronicler, Enguerrand de Monstrelet, provides a list of dead representing 335 individuals. Adding in others fatalities mentioned elsewhere, we can reach a total of 500, which must be taken as a minimum figure. Some of the dead were taken from the field for burial in their own lands (such as the Duke of Brabant), but others were buried in churches and monasteries in the area, such as at Auchy-lès-Hesdin. Although Monstrelet speaks of the digging of great grave pits near the field, these continue to elude detection. His figure of 5,800 buried therein is not credible.

Neither can we be sure about the number of English casualties. English chronicles give very low figures (between 30 and 100), but Burgundian texts suggest between 600 and 1,600. The financial records of the army cannot help since Henry decided subsequently that even those who died at the battle were entitled to pay for the whole campaign: therefore, they do not appear systematically in the post-campaign accounts. But it is obvious that very few English died compared with the French. This is important in terms of how the battle was fought and confirms the view that the French attack was undermined even before it was able to engage with the English men-at-arms. Had there been a high level of engagement, more English would have died.

French prisoners are well documented in the financial records since the king had a financial interest in the ransoms. Around 300 can be identified in such sources. As with the dead, most came from Picardy, Artois and Upper Normandy.

 ## EYEWITNESS ACCOUNTS OF THE BATTLE

There are several accounts of Agincourt in the chronicles of the early fifteenth century, though most are based on second-hand testimony. Five claim that the writer was present at the battle.

The anonymous author of *Gesta Henrici Quinti* (1417) was a priest attached to the royal household. His main purpose in writing the chronicle, which runs from Henry V's coronation on 9 April 1413 until the parliament of November 1416, was to glorify the king as a devout Christian prince blessed by the approval of God. The author was present throughout the 1415 expedition and so provides a comprehensive account of the campaign from the English perspective. He states he was on the battlefield, but that during the battle he was "sitting on a horse among the baggage at the rear of the battle". Therefore, despite being at Agincourt, it is doubtful he could see much with his own eyes. He was reliant on what participants in the engagement told him. But he probably wrote his account in 1417 at the latest, hence quite close in time to the events.

Another writer who claimed to be present was John Hardyng,

who wrote two versions of his chronicle in 1457 and 1464. By his own testimony, he claimed to have served with Sir Robert Umfraville on the 1415 campaign to France. Hardyng was born in the north of England, possibly Northumberland, in 1378. Yet, no evidence has been found for his participation in the expedition from the surviving muster rolls, nor of Umfraville, who seems rather to have been ordered to remain in England to defend the border against the Scots. Hardyng only mentions his own presence in the second version of his chronicle. It is questionable, therefore, whether he actually served on the campaign at all. Furthermore, both versions were written up more than 30 years after the battle, about which they have relatively little to say anyway.

Two further accounts are provided by Jean Waurin and Jean Le Fèvre (1444–60s), both writers from Picardy. According to Waurin, he was 15 at the time of the battle with the French army, whereas Févre was 19 and with the English army. It appears that Févre was in the service of the heralds, while it is unclear whether Waurin was a combatant or not. Both men, however, wrote their chronicles at least 30 years after the battle and drew heavily upon the account of the battle written by Enguerrand Monstrelet, whose chronicle was finished in 1447. This, together with the desire of the authors to present a pro-Burgundian account of events, means that their testimony needs to be treated with care.

The final eyewitness account is perhaps the most interesting since it is the recollection of a man captured at the battle – Ghillebert de Lannoy, Lord of Willerval. Ghillebert was 29 years old in 1415 and was the chamberlain to Philip, Count of Charolais (who was the eldest son of John the Fearless, Duke of Burgundy). He fought as a man-at-arms at the battle where he was wounded in the knee and the head, and left for dead. After being discovered among the bodies he was taken captive, and led to a house with 10 or 12 other prisoners who had all been wounded. Then, according to his account, a shout went up that the Duke of Brabant was making a new attack and that everyone should kill his prisoners. So that this could be done more quickly, the English set fire to the house where Ghillebert and the other prisoners were being held. Ghillebert managed to crawl out, only to be recaptured. He was subsequently sold to Sir John Cornwall and taken to England. A ransom of 1,200 crowns was demanded, but he was well treated and returned to France in 1416. Cornwall even gave him some money to purchase a new suit of armour.

 # THE BATTLEFIELD

No text makes it clear why the French had chosen Agincourt for battle. There had been action in this very area between the royal

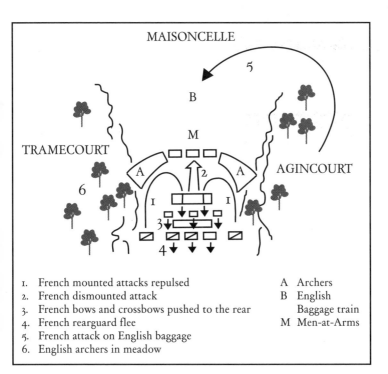

1. French mounted attacks repulsed
2. French dismounted attack
3. French bows and crossbows pushed to the rear
4. French rearguard flee
5. French attack on English baggage
6. English archers in meadow

A  Archers
B  English
   Baggage train
M  Men-at-Arms

army and the Duke of Burgundy in 1414, and therefore Constable d'Albret and others may have known the place already.

The seat of the battle is believed to lie between the villages of Agincourt and Tramecourt. Field-walking and metal-detecting in the area have so far failed to find any evidence of the battle, however. It is possible, therefore, that it was not fought here. Intriguingly, in the Cassini map of the second half of the eighteenth century, the battle is marked to the west of the village of Agincourt rather than to the east where the traditional site lies.

The battle is associated with Agincourt in the majority of early accounts. Monstrelet includes an explanation of its naming after the castle at Agincourt, a scene that found its way into Shakespeare. Some other names are found, however. Ghillebert de Lannoy, for instance, calls it the Battle of Ruisseauville.

# 8

# KEY PLAYERS

 EDWARD, DUKE OF YORK (C.1373–1415)

Edward of Langley, Duke of York was the most high profile English fatality at the battle. He was the eldest son of Edmund, fifth son of Edward III. He was close to Richard II, and accompanied the king on his expeditions to Ireland in 1394–95 and 1399. Despite this, he later provided significant service to his cousin, Henry Bolingbroke (Henry IV), after the latter usurped the throne in 1399. Although in the mid-1400s, the king had suspected Edward's loyalty, Prince Henry (the future Henry V) sprung to his defence and appears to have been a close ally. Edward dedicated to the prince his translation of the *Livre du chasse,* the hunting manual by Gaston Phébus, Count of Foix, adding personal elements of his own.

Edward's military service in these years included being the king's lieutenant in the duchy of Aquitaine and fighting the rebels in Wales. In 1412, he served on the expedition sent under the Duke of Clarence to assist the Armagnacs. On his return to England, in 1413, he passed by Paris where he saw the young Catherine de Valois and reported positively to the king about her beauty. After the accession of Henry V, he was a councillor of the king and was entrusted with diplomacy concerning France. His younger brother, Richard, Earl of Cambridge, was one of the conspirators executed in August 1415 for plotting to kill the king at Southampton, but Edward himself was not involved.

Since Edward was one of the leading peers of the realm and a close relative of the king, he was expected to raise a large retinue for the 1415 expedition. This comprised 400 men, made up of himself, one knight banneret, four knights bachelor, 94 men-at-arms and 300 archers. The majority of his retinue served at the battle, although 24 men were invalided home during the siege of Harfleur. According to several chronicle accounts, including *Gesta Henrici Quinti*, he was given command of the vanguard at the battle. This was a highly important and dangerous role since it involved facing the first assault of the French men-at-arms.

York was described in positive terms by chroniclers, especially by later Yorkist writers – as he was the great uncle of Edward IV – who gave a more prominent role to him in the battle. This included emphasizing his valiant death and attributing to him the idea of using stakes against the French cavalry. Edward's body was excarnated immediately after the battle by being boiled to remove the flesh. His bones were transported to England where he was buried at the Church of St Mary and All Saints in Fotheringhay, Northamptonshire. He had earlier founded a college of priests there. His will – written at Harfleur on 17 August – had stipulated burial "in the middle of the choir, near the steps, under a flat marble slab". The chancel was demolished in the Reformation, but a plaque in his memory was erected in 1573.

 ## SIR THOMAS ERPINGHAM (c.1355–1428)

Thomas Erpingham was born into an established east Anglian gentry family. As early as 1368, he accompanied his father to France in the service of Edward, the Black Prince. His career began in earnest when he served on a naval expedition in 1372. In 1379, we find him in the Calais garrison and in 1380, he became a retainer of John of Gaunt (at an annual fee of £20 in peace and

£33 6s 8d in war). Erpingham later accompanied Gaunt on the Scottish expedition in 1385 and to Castile the following year. He was also involved in the relief of Brest in 1385–86.

In 1390, Erpingham became a part of the household of Gaunt's son, Henry Bolingbroke, Earl of Derby, and served in the latter's expeditions to Prussia and Lithuania in the early 1390s – even accompanying Bolingbroke to the Holy Land in 1393. Following Bolingbroke's usurpation of the throne in 1399, Erpingham was well rewarded for his loyalty. He became a Knight of the Garter in 1401 and enjoyed appointments as steward of the royal household (1403–04) and Constable of Dover Castle and Warden of the Cinque Ports to 1409. In October 1404, he became acting Marshal of England and his services to the king and kingdom were later commended in parliament. During the reign of Henry V, he was appointed steward of the royal household, holding this role until May 1417. He was a member of the close royal circle and played a prominent role in the expedition of 1415. He was also a witness to the king's will made at Southampton on 27 July.

Erpingham indented to serve with a retinue of 80 men on the 1415 expedition, consisting of himself, two other knights, 17 men-at-arms and 60 archers. The company was mustered at Southampton Heath on 13 July by John Rothenale, controller of the royal household and the clerk John Strange. Although he seems to have been able to find only one knight for the campaign, Sir Walter Goldingham, two of his men-at-arms, Thomas Geney and John Calthorpe, were knights at the initial landing of the army in France. Three of the men-at-arms and two of the archers were invalided home during the course of the campaign, and another archer was killed on the march from Harfleur to Agincourt. Erpingham was present at Agincourt with 114 of his men, where one of the archers, Stephen Gerneyng, was killed during the engagement.

The mid-fifteenth century accounts of the Burgundian authors Monstrelet, Févre and Waurin describe Erpingham as being delegated by the king to draw up the formation of the troops:

he put the archers in the front and the men-at-arms behind them, creating two wings of men-at-arms and archers together. Furthermore, they describe him as giving a battle speech at the beginning of the battle on behalf of the king. Then, riding in front of the army, he threw his baton into the air shouting *"nescieque"*, an expression whose meaning remains unclear, but which seems to have been the signal for the attack to begin. These activities are not mentioned by fifteenth-century English sources. Erpingham died in 1428 and was buried at Norwich Cathedral, where he had previously funded the construction of a gate to the cathedral precinct that survives to this day. His effigy, once within the cathedral, now graces the gate into the Close.

 THOMAS, LORD CAMOYS (c.1350–1420/1)

Thomas, Lord Camoys was the son of John Camoys and the heir of his uncle, Thomas Camoys (d.1382). His first known military service occurred in 1380, when he took part in an expedition to France led by the fifth son of Edward III, Thomas of Woodstock, Earl of Buckingham, during which he was knighted by the latter. During the reign of Henry IV, he received a number of grants including the possession of Portchester Castle for life. He also served on a number of commissions of array in Surrey, Sussex and Southampton and escorted Henry's second wife, Joan of Navarre, from Brittany to England in 1403. In 1406, Camoys married Elizabeth Mortimer, the widow of Henry Percy (Hotspur) and herself a collateral member of the royal family. He was one of the councillors at the council on 16 April 1415 to plan the invasion of France. On 31 July, he was appointed as one of the commissioners who tried and condemned to death the Southampton plotters.

Camoys indented to serve with a retinue of 90 men on the 1415 expedition, consisting of himself, two knights bachelor, 27 men-at-arms and 60 archers. He lost at least four men-at-arms of his retinue because of the siege, either to death or being invalided home, but the remaining 86 were with him at the battle.

Camoys played an important role at Agincourt. The author of *Gesta Henrici Quinti* describes him as commander of the rearguard, the body of troops placed on the English left at the battle. He was one of the oldest participants and was obviously seen by Henry as a reliable commander, who could inspire his troops and keep them steady as the battle developed. The following year, he was rewarded by the king with his admission to the prestigious Order of the Garter. Camoys died in either 1420 or 1421 and was buried at St George's Church in Trotton, Sussex, where a fine brass survives of him and his wife Elizabeth: it portrays them holding hands, reflecting the height of fashion in monuments during this period.

## DAVY GAM (c.1380–1415)

Davy (or Dafydd) Gam came from a family which owed its prosperity to the Marcher Lords of Brecon, the Bohuns, and later the house of Lancaster. Along with his father and brothers, Gam served his Lancastrian lords faithfully during the course of the Welsh rebellion led by Owain Glyndŵr. His family was rewarded for this service by the receipt of lands confiscated from rebels in Cardiganshire and the lordship of Brecon. He did suffer harassment from former rebels in Wales, however, which culminated in his capture in 1412, for which he had to pay a heavy ransom to gain his freedom.

Gam indented to serve on the 1415 campaign as a man-at-arms with three archers. He died in the battle. Although his name is present in the list of dead as given by five chronicles, no details of the circumstances are given. Two of the five chronicles note his nationality: Peter Basset and Christopher Hanson call him "Davy Gam esquire, Welshman", and Adam Usk lists him as "David Gam of Brecon".

Various stories about Gam developed in later centuries. According to Sir Walter Raleigh's *History of the World* (1614), Henry V sent Gam to spy on the French. He returned to tell the king that, "of the *Frenchmen*, there were enough to be killed; enough to be taken prisoners; and enough to run away". This story was developed further in Michael Drayton's poem of 1627, "The Bataille of Agincourt". Wynne's expansion in 1697 of David Powel's *History of Cambria* (1584) added the notion that he was knighted at the battle as he lay dying. In later centuries, the myth of a posthumous dubbing to knighthood developed. Similarly, a long-running tradition, expressed for instance by the Carmarthenshire poet Lewis Glyn Cothi, states that Gam was knighted prior to the battle, but no contemporary evidence of this exists.

 ## MARSHAL BOUCICAUT (1366–1421)

Jean II Le Meingre (later known as Marshal Boucicaut) had followed his distinguished father into military service, being dubbed a knight before the Battle of Roosebeke on 27 November 1382 (even though he was only 16 at this juncture). He became famous through his participation in crusading activity and diplomacy, as well as the Anglo–French wars. We find him serving with the Teutonic order in their crusade against the pagan Lithuanians and then subsequently in Hungary, Constantinople and even the court of the Sultan.

In 1391, Boucicaut was appointed Marshal of France by Charles VI. That he was still only 26 years old shows how strong a reputation he had already developed and also that he was seen as a worthy heir to his father (who had held the office of marshal in the past). The long truce between England and France from 1396 enabled Boucicaut to continue his crusading career. In particular, we find him at the Battle of Nicopolis (25 September), where the Ottoman forces decisively defeated the Christian army. He survived the battle and in thanksgiving founded the chivalric order of *L'Escu vert à la Dame Blanche* ("The Green Shield of the White Lady") to protect women who had lost their loved ones in the battle.

Boucicaut continued in action in Asia Minor during the late 1390s. In 1401, he was appointed Governor of Genoa by Charles VI, a not wholly successful endeavour as Boucicaut's actions triggered rebellion. We know that he was already respected as an embodiment of chivalry and he participated in various important international jousts. His career was celebrated in a work written in 1409: the *Livre des fais du bon messire Jehan Le Maingre* (the book of deeds of the good monsieur Jean le Meingre).

Boucicaut was fully involved in reconnoitring against the English during the siege of Harfleur and in shadowing the English army as it marched towards and then along the Somme. He helped draw up a proposed French plan of battle around this time, expecting to fight the English in the Somme valley. Captured at the Battle of Agincourt, he was taken to England. It proved impossible to negotiate a ransom settlement and the English were keen to keep him in close custody. He died in England, most probably at Robert Waterton's seat at Methley, on 25 June 1421. His body was taken back to France and buried at Tours.

 ## CHARLES, DUKE OF ORLÉANS (1394–1465)

The most high-status prisoner taken at Agincourt, Charles of Orléans was the nephew of the French king. He was the eldest son of Louis, Duke of Orléans, younger brother of Charles VI. A feud developed between Duke Louis and his cousin John the Fearless, Duke of Burgundy, over control of the government in the early fifteenth century, in the light of Charles VI's madness. Duke John arranged the assassination of Duke Louis in Paris on 23 November 1407.

Initially, the young Duke Charles had little choice but to accept Duke John's power and to enter into a supposed reconciliation.

But in 1410, he married the daughter of Bernard, Count of Armagnac as part of the building up of a stronger opposition against the Burgundians. In 1410–12, there was effectively civil war between the two factions and supporters of Duke Charles were known as the Armagnacs. In 1412, his group approached Henry IV for military aid, promising to assist him in return in efforts to recover his French lands. Over subsequent years, the Duke of Burgundy fell from power and Charles of Orléans was involved in war against him. On 4 September 1414, the two parties were reconciled, although there were still fears that the old feud would reopen.

Initially, in the face of English invasion in 1415, it was decided that both the Duke of Orléans and the Duke of Burgundy should send 500 men-at-arms to the French army but not come in person. Subsequently, however, it was decided by the king and dauphin that Duke Charles should join with the French army. Thus, we find him at Agincourt. He was probably dubbed a knight on the eve or morning of the battle, where he held the main command despite his lack of experience. He fought in the vanguard and was found lying under a heap of dead after the first phase of the battle. As a prisoner, he was taken to England and was not ransomed until 1440. Henry V had advised on his deathbed against Charles's release. While in England, the duke wrote poetry in both English and French. He did not play much of a role in French politics or military activity in the 25 years after his return to France, but at the failure of the senior French line in 1498, his son became king as Louis XII (d. 1515).

##  ANTHONY, DUKE OF BRABANT (1384–1415)

Anthony was one of the French casualties of the Battle of Agincourt, alongside his younger brother, Philip, Count of Nevers and Rethel. He was the second son of Philip the Bold, Duke of Burgundy (one of the sons of King John II of France).

The Burgundian collateral line of the royal family was extremely important, especially in the light of the struggle for control of the French government in the wake of Charles VI's madness. Anthony's elder brother, John the Fearless, Duke of Burgundy from 1404, was highly influential, controlling the king for most of the period to 1414 when he fell from favour. In the civil war between the Burgundians and their opponents, the Armagnacs, Anthony played the role of peacemaker.

Anthony had become governor in 1404 and subsequently, in 1406, Duke of Brabant (through inheritance from his mother's aunt). His territory, focused on the three great towns of Brussels, Antwerp and Maastricht, was extensive and wealthy, and he did much to extend his power and financial income. The duke's marriage, in 1409, to the niece of the King of Bohemia, Wenceslaus IV of Luxembourg, also gave him the governorship of the duchy of Luxembourg from 1412.

According to his secretary, Emond de Dynter (who wrote a chronicle of the Dukes of Brabant), Duke Anthony received letters at Louvain on 21 October telling him of the impending battle and urging him to set out in person. He immediately ordered letters to be sent to his own nobles, officials and towns so that they could follow him with their troops. On the morning of 25 October, however, he was still at Lens in Artois, probably expecting that battle was to be given at Aubigny-en-Artois. However, a messenger came telling him the English were to be fought before midday, at Agincourt. Therefore he made haste to get there but arrived late, having travelled 116 miles (186 km) over the previous 48 hours.

According to Dynter, the duke had to borrow the armour of his chamberlain, and, not having his own coat of arms, he cut a hole in a flag of one of his trumpeters and put it over his head. This situation may have contributed to his not being recognized and therefore killed rather than being taken prisoner. According to the reminiscence of Ghillebert de Lannoy, who had fought on the French side and was captured in the first phase of the battle, the arrival of the Duke of Brabant was also the occasion for Henry's order to kill the prisoners. The duke's servants found his body on the field and took it back to his duchy, where after a funeral in Brussels it was buried in the church of Saint-Jean of Tervuren. Financial records show that 17 of his men died at the battle. We do not know how many troops he had managed to bring: only 37 are known by name. Antwerp provided 57 archers, but there is uncertainty over whether they reached the battle in time.

# 9

# THE AFTERMATH OF AGINCOURT

 NEWS OF THE BATTLE

On Friday 25 October 1415, "a lamentable report, replete with sadness, and cause for endless sorrow, had alarmed the community throughout all the City". This was a rumour, recorded in the official records of the city known as the *Letter-Books*, that the movements of the king and his army "lay shrouded in mystery". The citizens were "ardently athirst, in expectation to hear some encouraging news of the success of the royal expedition". This was to come four days later.

News of the battle reached London on the morning of 29 October. According to the *Chronicle of London* (written in the late fifteenth century), this information arrived while the population were still asleep in their beds. The citizens of London then went to all of the city churches and rang all of their bells in celebration exclaiming the hymn "*Te Deum laudamus*" (O God, we praise you).

An entry in *Letter-Book I* describes what happened next:

> "*And on the morrow of the Apostles Simon and Jude, the said Nicholas Wotton, Mayor, and the Aldermen, together with an immense number of the Commonalty*

> *of the citizens of the city aforesaid, going on pilgrimage, went on foot to Westminster, and, having first made devout thanksgiving, with due solemnity, in the Minster there, for the joyous news that had then arrived, the said Nicholas Wotton was by the said Aldermen and Commonalty presented before the Barons of the Exchequer of our Lord the King, at Westminster, admitted, and sworn."*

According to the *Chronicle of London*, the citizens then returned home on horseback "and were joyful and glad for the good tiding that they had of the king, and thanked our lord Jesus Christ, his mother Saint Mary, and Saint George, and all the holy company of heaven and said "Hec est dies quam fecit" (This is the day which the Lord hath made).

The entry in the *Letter-Book* makes clear that the pilgrimage on foot was not to set a precedent (it was customary to ride in state on such occasions). Instead, this was an exceptional set of circumstances created by the joy experienced by the citizens at hearing news of the victory after previous bad tidings. Furthermore, the pilgrimage was to honour God and his saints, particularly that of St Edward the Confessor whose shrine was at Westminster Abbey.

 ## THE KING'S ENTRY INTO LONDON

Henry V did not rush to return to England after his victory at Agincourt. He arrived at Calais on 29 October, but did not land back at Dover until 16 November. While he was absent, parliament met at Westminster between 4 and 13 November, one of the shortest parliaments on record. The chancellor's opening speech emphasized Henry's recent victories, but also his need for more money in order to ensure similar successes in the future. Henry may even have been contemplating immediate military action, perhaps aimed at capturing the town of Ardres on the edge of the Calais march or at least that was the impression he wanted to give in order to encourage the Commons' generosity. He was not disappointed. They agreed to bring forward by two months the instalment of the lay subsidy due for collection in February 1416. They also granted a further lay subsidy for collection in November as well as giving the king the wool subsidy and tonnage and poundage for life. Usually kings had to ask each parliament for the right to collect such tolls.

Three days after parliament closed, Henry arrived in England to much rejoicing. He passed through Canterbury en route to London in order to give thanks for his victory at the shrine of Thomas Becket. The delay in his return had allowed the city of London time to organize a great pageant to welcome him.

On the morning of Saturday 23 November, the mayor and the 24 aldermen went out to meet the king at Blackheath, as was their custom. At London Bridge, the king was greeted by symbols of the city's authority, statues of a giant and his wife (Gog and Magog), surrounded by royal flags and with the legend "*Civitas Regis Iustitice*" (the City of the King of Justice), a quotation from Exodus. Henry's own power was reflected in statues of an antelope (one of his badges) bearing a sceptre, and a lion holding a royal standard unfurled. A choir of boys greeted him with "Blessed is He who comes in the Name of the Lord". In Cornhill, a wooden tower had been constructed with the arms of St George, St Edmund, St Edward and England. As the king passed, men dressed in white robes let loose birds that flew down onto the king, all to the sound of psalms. Yet another tower at the entrance to Cheapside bore the city's arms and contained men dressed as the apostles, English kings, and saints, which delivered to the king leaves of silver and morsels of bread symbolizing the Mass, with wine pouring out of the conduit.

The cross at Cheapside had been converted into a castle, again with the royal arms and with a choir of beautiful young maidens singing "Welcome Henry the Fifth, king of England and of France". It is possible that their song was what is now known as the "Agincourt Carol", which urged England to give thanks to God for such a king. A further tower greeted the king near St Pauls, this time reflecting the splendour of heaven. The streets were packed with citizens keen to see and applaud their king, who gave thanks at St Paul's Cathedral before making his way to Westminster Abbey to give thanks there. This was by no means a Roman-style triumph. Henry had with him only a small retinue of his closest household. But he did have with him the six principal French prisoners under a guard of knights.

 ## THE FATE OF THE FRENCH PRISONERS

The fate of the French prisoners taken at Agincourt depended upon their rank and wealth. The majority of the prisoners, including many of low status, were soon released, whereas a small number of high-profile noblemen languished for years in captivity in England. Those prisoners who survived the massacre at the end of the battle had been escorted to Calais with the rest of the English army. There, according to the Burgundian chroniclers Fèvre and Waurin, some prisoners were sold by soldiers to the merchants and leading citizens of the town for a low price, or even in return for food. This was because the English soldiers were barred access to Calais and were said to be in desperate straits. Many of the French prisoners were therefore never taken to England. Others were subsequently given safe conducts to return to France to collect their ransoms, or else arranged for their servants to bring them funds.

The highest status French prisoners, however, stayed in captivity, even if that was relatively comfortable, because of their potential political value. The "big six" were Charles, Duke of Orléans (see pages 93–94); Jean de Clermont, Duke of Bourbon; Louis de Bourbon, Count of Vendôme; Charles of Artois, Count of Eu; Arthur of Brittany, Count of Richemont; and the Marshal of France, Jean II le Meingre (known as Boucicaut, see pages 92–93). As high-ranking French noblemen, they could be expected to command large ransoms, but none of them was important enough to force the French Crown to the negotiating table. Even so, Henry tried to persuade the Duke of Bourbon to accept him as King of France. Arthur of Brittany agreed to do so after the Treaty of Troyes and was released from his captivity, serving the English cause until he returned to the allegiance of Charles VII in 1424. On his deathbed, Henry ordered that Orléans and Bourbon should remain captives until his son, Henry VI, came of age. Boucicaut died in English captivity in 1421 and Bourbon in 1434. Vendôme and Eu were released in a complicated exchange for English prisoners captured in the wars of the 1420s and 30s. Orléans was held as a prisoner for 25 years and was only released for a ransom of £30,000 in 1440 in an attempt to promote peace with Charles VII, King of France.

## FRENCH EFFORTS TO RETAKE HARFLEUR, 1416

Agincourt was not a decisive victory. It was a great boost to Henry's position at home, but it had not forced the French to the negotiating table. None of the prisoners, not even the king's nephew, the Duke of Orléans, was politically significant enough to oblige the French to do so. Charles VI had wisely kept away from personal involvement in military action against the English.

Even after the victory at Agincourt, Henry's conquest – Harfleur – needed to maintain its large garrison of 1,200 men. As an outpost in hostile territory, it was extremely difficult to supply. This prompted its captain, Thomas Beaufort, Earl of Dorset, to conduct forays into the surrounding area in search of food. One of these ended in near disaster in March 1416, with English losses of men and horses. It was already apparent that the French would attempt to retake the town. Even before Christmas 1415, they had approached the Genoese for 20 galleys to blockade the town from the sea. The ships arrived in April, as did troops installed in various locations encircling Harfleur.

On 14 April 1416, the Earl of Dorset wrote to the royal council explaining that he would not be able to hold out much longer because his men were so short of food. Supplies were despatched, but it was apparent that an army needed to be sent to relieve the town. Over the following months, 7,300 troops were raised in England. The king initially intended to lead the expedition in person, but since he was busy entertaining Emperor Sigismund –who had come to England, ostensibly as a possible mediator between England and France – command was given to Henry's second brother, John, Duke of Bedford.

The army had a ratio of one man-at-arms to two archers, the customary ratio for naval campaigns (as opposed to the one to three seen in land campaigns, as in most retinues for the 1415 campaign). Archers were deemed less useful for fighting from ships. On 15 August, the English naval force defeated the French and Genoese force in the mouth of the Seine. This victory was a further sign of God's support for Henry and for his ambitions in France. The author of *Gesta Henrici Quinti* waxed as lyrically about it as the victory at Agincourt. Indeed, without the successful defence of Harfleur, it would have been impossible for Henry to launch another major campaign in the summer of 1417 aimed at the conquest of Normandy. As a result of his endeavours in holding Harfleur, Thomas Beaufort was created Duke of Exeter at the parliament that met in October to November 1416 (and which voted Henry a double lay subsidy to support the costs of his planned expedition).

 ## THE CONQUEST OF NORMANDY, 1417–19

In the spring of 1417, Henry began to raise an army of around 10,000 men for 12 months' service in France. Most of the indentures were sealed in early February, and in general followed the ratio of one man-at-arms to three archers (which had predominated in 1415). On this occasion the landing was in Lower Normandy, south of the Seine estuary. It was deliberately arranged for 1 August 1417, the feast of St Peter ad Vincula perhaps being chosen to symbolize Henry's intention to liberate the Normans from the chains of French rule. Certainly, before too long – if not right from the start – Henry began to call himself Duke of Normandy (alongside his title King of France), and to exploit for propaganda purposes the old links between England and Normandy dating back to 1066.

The landing site at the mouth of the river Touques had been chosen to give an easier bridgehead than in 1415. Once the coastal area to east and west had been secured, Henry moved on to besiege Caen, which surrendered after two weeks (thanks to heavy bombardment) and subsequently became the centre of Henry's administration.

The king then moved directly south, capturing towns and castles as he went in order to cut Lower Normandy in two. Falaise held out for 10 weeks, but once it was in Henry's hands in February 1418, he was able to divide his army, sending his brother of Clarence east towards Lisieux and his brother of Gloucester westwards towards the Cotentin.

By the summer of 1418, enough territory in Lower Normandy was in English hands to allow Henry to begin the siege of Rouen in August 1418. The city surrendered in January 1419, thereby becoming the largest place successfully taken by siege across the whole of the Hundred Years War. That the French had not been able to send a relief force was testimony to the impact of Agincourt – they were reluctant to face the English in battle again – and to the grave divisions within French politics. In the summer of 1418, the Duke of Burgundy had seized Paris and control of the king, forcing the dauphin Charles (who had seen the death of two of his elder brothers over the preceding years, Louis in December 1415 and John in April 1417) to flee south of the Loire. The Armagnac party, of which the dauphin was now the nominal leader, had been much damaged, not least by the capture of the Dukes of Orléans and Bourbon at Agincourt.

The surrender of Rouen had a domino effect on the rest of Upper Normandy, which fell into Henry's hands with little resistance, enabling him to begin to move towards Paris. The French Crown, under Burgundian influence, was keen to negotiate: in meetings held with Henry at Meulan, where he first met Princess Catherine, a settlement was almost reached that would have given him Normandy and a French marriage, as well as lands of the Brétigny settlement of 1360.

One last effort was made by the two French factions to unite against the English. On 10 September 1419, an act of reconciliation was planned for the dauphin, Charles and John the Fearless, Duke of Burgundy, on the bridge at Montereau, but instead the dauphin's henchmen assassinated the duke. This inevitably threw the new Duke of Burgundy, Philip, into an alliance with Henry, as well as opening up for the English king an opportunity to propose a settlement that would in effect make the French accept his claim to the throne.

 # THE TREATY OF TROYES, 1420

Over the months that followed the murder of Duke John of Burgundy, Henry V put forward a proposal that he should become King of France at the death of Charles VI. After much diplomatic to-ing and fro-ing, the French royal government, still under Burgundian control, accepted these terms. Key elements were the desire of the Burgundians for revenge against the dauphin, and the fear of the Parisians that if Henry did not get his way, he would attack the French capital. On 21 May 1420, the treaty was sealed in the cathedral of Troyes, and on 2 June, Henry married Catherine. For Henry, the treaty was a triumph: realistically he could never have had his claim accepted without the acceptance of the French king. Furthermore, in the light of Charles's mental condition, the treaty made him regent: therefore he was already king in all but name. But while the dauphin lived, there would be many who would contest the legitimacy of his exclusion.

The treaty placed on Henry an obligation to restore to royal obedience all lands and peoples who followed the Armagnac or Dauphinist party. Therefore, although it was portrayed as a settlement to end Anglo–French hostilities and to unite the two kingdoms under the same king, it promised further war within the kingdom itself. The remainder of Henry V's life was largely spent in military action besieging places around Paris that continued to support the dauphin. Although Henry succeeded in his sieges, his eldest brother, Thomas, Duke of Clarence, was killed in action at the Battle of Baugé on 21 March 1421, a sign that it would not be easy to establish the double monarchy outside the areas controlled by the English and their Burgundian allies.

 JOAN OF ARC

On 31 August 1422, Henry V died at the Chateau of Vincennes to the east of Paris. Less than two months later, on 21 October 1422, Charles VI died. The new king of the double monarchy established by the Treaty of Troyes was a baby – Henry VI was only nine months old at his father's death. His uncle John, Duke of Bedford, became Regent of France.

There were some notable military successes in the 1420s, especially battle victories at Cravant on 31 July 1423 and Verneuil on 16 August 1424 (the latter often being considered a second Agincourt, not least because of English arrow power). English armies advanced into Maine, and, in late 1428, began a big push towards the Loire with the city of Orléans as the main target. The dauphin, with his bases at Chinon and Tours, was under threat.

The siege of Orléans proved difficult. Its commander, Thomas, Earl of Salisbury, was killed early in the siege by a gunshot.

Relations with the Burgundians were also less harmonious than in the past. But the crucial reverse followed the inspirational involvement of Joan of Arc. Promising the dauphin, Charles, a sign, she was able to enter Orléans. By early May 1429, Joan and an army sent by Charles were able to force the English to raise their siege. On 18 June, the French defeated the English in battle at Patay, going on to retake many towns, including the coronation city of Reims. It was there, on 16 July 1429, that the dauphin was crowned Charles VII. The English retaliated by having Henry VI crowned in November 1429 in England and in December 1431 in Paris. But even though Joan had fallen into their hands and had been tried for heresy and burned at Rouen on 30 May 1431, the English never fully recovered from the losses of 1429–31. By September 1435, the Duke of Bedford was dead and Philip, Duke of Burgundy had transferred his allegiance to Charles VII.

 ## ENGLISH DEFEAT AND EXPULSION FROM FRANCE, 1449–53

By the turn of 1435, the Treaty of Troyes had failed. In the following May, the English lost control of Paris to Charles VI and fell back on Normandy and Maine. Even here they were suffering losses: most of Upper Normandy, including Henry V's first conquest of Harfleur, fell to the French. Although Harfleur was recovered in 1440, Dieppe remained in French hands. By 1444, the impasse was obvious and Henry VI, never particularly enthusiastic about the wars, was keen to come to a truce that involved his marriage to Margaret of Anjou. Charles VII took advantage of the truce to reform his army, and in particular to build up the *francs archers*, longbowmen imitative of the English model. In 1449, he invaded the duchy of Normandy and conquered it in even less time than it had taken Henry V in 1417–19.

As in 1419, the fall of Rouen (November 1449) triggered the collapse of the rest of the duchy. A final battle victory for Charles at Formigny on 15 April 1450 sealed the fate of the duchy. By mid-August, the last English toehold at Cherbourg fell. Gascony fell over the next year, although a rebellion in Bordeaux briefly restored English control until the victory of the French at the Battle of Castillon on 17 July 1453. Calais remained in English hands until 1558, but the hopes of a double monarchy of England and France, or even of the restoration of the Plantagenet landholdings, were a dead letter once Normandy and Gascony had fallen to Charles VII. The reversal of English fortunes triggered civil war in the Wars of the Roses.

# 10

# MEDIEVAL WARFARE

 CHEVAUCHÉES

One of the most common methods of warfare during the Hundred Years War was carrying out raids into enemy territory known as chevauchées. This was a tactic particularly favoured by the English in the fourteenth century, although it was also employed at times during the fifteenth century too.

Armies carrying out chevauchées were entirely mounted to allow them to move quickly across enemy territory. They were not concerned with besieging large towns or gaining territory through conquest. Instead, the purpose was to inflict as much destruction as possible in the countryside. This involved burning crops, sacking small and undefended settlements, taking prisoners and putting people to the sword. It was, therefore, a form of economic warfare designed to reduce the willingness and ability of a people to resist their enemies. A ruler who allowed his subjects to suffer in such a way lost prestige, whereas the commander of successful raids could gain much renown.

Chevauchées could also be highly profitable enterprises with large quantities of loot gained, such as during the Black Prince's chevauchées of 1355 and 1356. The success of this method of warfare relied upon a willingness to give or seek battle. English victories at Crécy (1346) and Poitiers (1356) meant that the

French were reluctant to confront their opponents in the field and to contest their raids into France. However, these raids proved to be a largely ineffective method for taking territory. Chevauchées also ran the risk of being attacked by enemy armies; at Poitiers, the Black Prince was able to defeat a French royal army but, in 1421, a chevauchée led by the Duke of Clarence, brother of Henry V, into Maine was defeated at the Battle of Baugé.

 # BATTLES

Battles rarely took place in medieval warfare, which was instead largely characterized by raids and sieges. This was because offering battle was risky and could have decisive consequences. At the Battle of Agincourt, many of the most prominent noblemen in France were killed or captured, which damaged the prestige of the French nation; in contrast, Henry V's reputation was greatly enhanced. On other occasions, the consequences could be even more significant. The capture of John II at the Battle of Poitiers (1356) meant that the English were able to enter into the negotiations that led to the Treaty of Brétigny (1360) from a position of strength. Earlier, in 1066, the Battle of Hastings had resulted in the death of King Harold Godwin and the conquest of England by William, Duke of Normandy.

The outcome of the best-known battles of the Hundred Years War – Crécy, Poitiers and Agincourt – were determined in large part by the English use of the longbow. This was particularly effective against cavalry, whose horses were lightly armoured, if at all. At Crécy in particular, the arrows shot by the English archers severely disrupted the French mounted charges. This was not an infallible weapon, however, as the French were later able to win decisive victories against English armies at the battles of Patay (1429) and Formigny (1450). Battles were often decided as a result of the melee, when both armies engaged in hand-to-hand fighting. It was during this stage of the action that the prowess of the heavily armoured men-at-arms often proved to be decisive. At Agincourt, the success of the English men-at-arms against their French opponents was a key element in the outcome of the battle.

#  NAVAL WARFARE

The need to transport armies by sea across the Channel meant that naval warfare played an important role in the Hundred Years War. This took the form of large-scale naval battles, small naval engagements and coastal raids. During this period, a royal navy as such did not exist and, with the king owning only a small number of ships, requisitioned merchant vessels made up the bulk of naval expeditions.

As on land, naval battles were comparatively rare events; this was in large part due to the difficulties of locating an enemy fleet, particularly while at sea. This meant that battles tended to occur in or near harbours, such as at the battles of Sluys (1340), Winchelsea (1350) and La Rochelle (1372). These contests at times involved hundreds of ships, as well as thousands of sailors and soldiers. Vessels were sometimes sunk during these battles, mainly as a result of ramming, but the primary objective was to capture enemy ships by killing their crews. On occasion, large numbers of vessels could be captured in this way, with perhaps as many as 190 ships captured by the English at the Battle of Sluys. Battles at sea were rarely decisive, however, as the lack of a large permanent navy meant that it was not possible to prevent enemy fleets from sailing.

The weapons used in naval warfare were mostly the same as those used on land, since battles were fought by bringing the ships together and fighting hand to hand. This included melee weapons, such as swords and poleaxes, as well as missile weapons, such as longbows, crossbows and guns. A small number of specialized naval weapons also existed, however, such as spears called "gads" and darts, which were thrown onto enemy decks. Fleets were also used to launch raids on coastal communities during the Hundred Years War, with a number of places attacked, pillaged and burned, including Southampton (1338), the Isle of Wight (1376), Rye (1377) and Winchelsea (1380).

# CASTLES AND FORTIFICATIONS

The high frequency of sieges in medieval warfare was due to the large numbers of walled towns and castles in Europe. Towns that lacked defences were vulnerable to being sacked by enemy armies, which is why large sums of money were spent on fortifications. At the most basic level, this could consist of a ditch or a wall made out of earth. By contrast, more sophisticated defences incorporated large stone walls, towers and gatehouses. These could be very costly to erect, both in terms of money and manpower, which is why kings often provided financial support to towns for building fortifications. In England, some towns were given the right to levy a tax on merchants trading goods in a settlement – known as murage – for the construction and repair of town walls. The development of gunpowder weapons meant that changes occurred to town defences in the late fourteenth and fifteenth centuries, with the addition of gun-loops and specialized outworks known as bulwarks, for the deployment of guns.

The other major form of fortification in the Middle Ages was the castle. This was a fortified structure belonging to the king or nobility, located in the countryside or in an urban settlement. Castles played an important part in warfare; not only did they provide a passive defensive role in protecting a particular location, but they also played an offensive role, as a heavily defended safe base from which the garrison could control the surrounding countryside. This is why invaders often felt obliged to besiege castles, because an area could not be fully controlled unless they were captured. By the fifteenth century, castles on both sides of the

Channel were mostly made out of stone and, in addition to their military role, also served as palaces, estate centres and prisons.

 # LOGISTICS

Logistics were vital to the conduct of warfare in the Middle Ages, as armies could not fight without being paid or supplied with victuals and equipment. During the start of the Hundred Years War, soldiers served in return for pay as opposed to carrying out unpaid feudal service. This meant that large sums of money needed to be raised in advance by the government. It also meant that clerks had to be employed to ensure that these men received payment and to make sure that fraud did not take place. It is due to the survival of a large proportion of the records that they created, such as muster rolls, that the names of many of the English soldiers who served in the Hundred Years War have survived.

English armies that campaigned in France also had to be transported by sea. This at times placed huge strains on English shipping, as it could take hundreds of vessels to transport thousands of men, horses and equipment to the Continent. On campaign, soldiers were sometimes expected to live off the land in enemy territory, particularly during chevauchées. This could be risky, however, as it was not always possible to safely obtain sufficient supplies of food and it antagonized the local population. It was often necessary, therefore, to purchase large quantities of victuals from merchants to ensure that the soldiers in armies were adequately fed. This also applied to the garrisons of towns and castles, with Calais almost entirely dependent on imports of food and other supplies from England.

# MILITARY INTELLIGENCE

The ability to effectively wage war in the Middle Ages depended then – as it does now – on reliable intelligence. This included gathering information on the movements of enemy armies and fleets, the strength of fortifications and other activities. Mounted scouts would be used on campaign to ride ahead of an army to ensure that it was not attacked unawares. The expertise of sailors and foreign merchants could also be utilized to gain intelligence about enemy coastal communities and defences. This was particularly useful when armies were transported to potentially hostile landing sites as opposed to friendly ports – as was the case in 1415, when the English disembarked in Normandy near to the town of Harfleur.

Spies were also regularly employed for gathering information. On occasion, these agents could reveal valuable intelligence. Measures taken to prevent spies from revealing sensitive information included orders to close the ports. For instance, in 1346, Edward III ordered that no one should leave England until eight days after the departure of his expedition, for fear that spies would reveal that Normandy was its destination. Additional intelligence could also be provided by envoys engaged in diplomatic missions. In 1415, Henry V was able to benefit from the information provided by men he had sent to France as ambassadors, such as Sir William Bourchier and Bishop Courtenay, as to the strength of the town of Harfleur.

# SIEGE WARFARE

The economic and strategic value of towns and castles meant that they were often the targets of enemy attacks. In many cases, however, sieges were not undertaken by armies – this was either because the fortifications were judged to be too difficult to attack, or alternatively because the garrison decided that they had little chance of being relieved, so agreed to surrender under terms. In the latter case, garrisons were often allowed to leave unmolested with their weapons in return for their surrender. Linked to this was an arrangement, known as a composition, whereby garrisons agreed to surrender after a certain number of days if they were not relieved by a friendly army that came to their rescue. Garrisons were often prepared to surrender, particularly if they calculated that they could not resist a siege. During the medieval period, if attackers successfully captured a town or castle without the garrison surrendering on terms, then they were entitled to kill the defenders. In those situations, only the wealthiest defenders would be captured for ransom, with the common soldiers and civilians at the mercy of the victors.

However, when the garrison of a settlement refused to surrender, the attackers were forced to take more active measures. At the most basic level, this involved blockading the settlement so that the garrison was unable to bring in supplies such as food. This was often one of the best ways to capture a town or castle, as the attackers did not have to risk casualties in attempting an assault – starvation would eventually force the garrison to surrender. Sometimes more direct methods were used by besiegers. These included the use of siege weapons to attempt to gain entrance to a settlement, either through using ladders, or by using artillery that could cause damage to the walls. The latter included stone-throwing weapons such as trebuchets, bolt-throwing springalds and guns.

 # THE RULES OF WAR

Medieval warfare was certainly brutal by modern standards but it was not entirely unregulated. The shared values of the aristocratic warrior elite, known as chivalry, meant that it was expected that certain practices would be observed in wartime. These included taking enemy combatants prisoner for ransom, and the protection of women and the poor. These ideals were not always realized in practice, but they did serve to temper some of the more savage aspects of warfare. Efforts were also made to control the behaviour of soldiers while serving on campaigns. In England, these took the form of military ordinances issued by the king, the earliest surviving example of which dates from 1385 during the reign of Richard II. Some variation occurred over time, but these ordinances typically included clauses that related to obeying orders, the protection of church property and women, keeping watch when required to do so and to only leave the army on the march with permission. The need to maintain military discipline meant that the punishment meted out for infringing these instructions was often the death penalty.

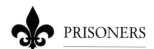 PRISONERS

Defeated soldiers, who were unable or unwilling to flee from attackers, were not always killed but were sometimes taken prisoner. The motive for taking enemy combatants captive, as opposed to killing them, was often based on financial considerations. High-status aristocratic prisoners could command hefty ransoms in return for their freedom while even comparatively low-status soldiers could be of some value. This is reflected in the comments made by the chronicler Jean Froissart that the English soldiers who took part in the Battle of Poitiers (1356) "became rich in honour and possessions, as much from the ransoms of captives as from the gain of gold and silver found there". Prisoners were often held by their captives according to their station in life or alternatively were held in war prisons, until their ransoms were paid. Some of these men were given safe conducts to their homes to collect this money in person, whereas others relied on their families or servants to do this on their behalf. The English and French Crowns also had an interest in the ransoming of enemy combatants as they were entitled to a share of the proceeds.

# 11

# ARMS

 ## MAKERS OF WEAPONS

The huge requirement for weapons for military service during the fourteenth century resulted in the migration of arms makers to London. The role of the Tower of London, and the office of the Privy Wardrobe within it, as the principal armoury of England encouraged its suppliers to cluster round the Tower. Many workmen were employed directly, and manufactured arms within the Tower. Others supplied arms to order. By the third quarter of the fourteenth century, they had begun to form trade companies or guilds, which became increasingly specialized: for example, in 1371, the bowyer and fletcher John Patyn was forced to choose which of these trades he would follow.

The bowyers established workshops in Bowyers Row, just to the west of St Paul's, and by 1399 their reputation was such that several bowyers, including Thomas Coton and William Morris, and the master of the fletchers, Stephen Seder, were commissioned by Henry IV to survey the Tower armoury for the disposal of redundant and defective arms. We know from the Privy Wardrobe accounts that fletchers were paid 6d a day like most skilled workmen of the period and could assemble nearly 200 arrows a day. The longbowstringmakers formed their own guild and many craftsmen, known only as John, Thomas, Randolph or William

Stringer, produced longbow strings for the Tower by the gross (i.e. 144 items).

While archery equipment was entirely English, edged weapons were often sourced abroad. The repair of a number of Henry V's swords in the period around the Agincourt campaign shows that they, or at least their blades, were from Passau in Bavaria. Other German centres, such as Solingen, were a significant source of blades throughout western Europe. Guns of bronze were cast for the Tower by London braziers from the middle of the fourteenth century. By the end of the century, there were numerous London specialists, such as John Molling, William Fungry and William Woodward, who specialized in cast-bronze guns, and smiths like Stephen atte Mersh and William Byker, who were making iron guns. Other craftsmen specialized in the manufacture and supply of gunpowder for the artillery (see Chapter 13).

 THE SWORD

The knightly sword, formed of a straight, double-edged blade, with a cross guard, single-handed grip and counterbalancing pommel, evolved rapidly during the early fourteenth century in response to evolutions in armour. The blade acquired a sharp point, probably for directing thrusts into the gaps in plate armour. As the shield disappeared from the equipment of the fully armoured man-at-arms in the middle of the fourteenth century, the hilt became extended so that the sword could be wielded in two hands. By the second decade of the fifteenth century, we find swords with cross guards fitted with a finger loop – this protected the index finger when it was wrapped around the blade to enable more accurately directed thrusts. The science of fencing had its beginnings in the previous century with the production of fight manuals. These show that swords, especially when used in conjunction with full armour, were used in a wide variety of ways, the pommels used for pummelling, the guards as hooks to drag down an opponent's blade and the blades themselves gripped with the left hand and used as a spear. In noble and royal circles, swords were often lavishly decorated, their hilts and scabbards covered in velvet or coloured leather, and their belts adorned with silver, gilt or enamelled fittings.

Daggers in north-west Europe were carried by the knightly classes and common soldiers alike. There were three main forms popular in England and France during the early fifteenth century: the quillon dagger, with a cross guard like a small version of the knightly sword; the rondel dagger, which had a pair of discs at either end of the grip forming pommel and guard; and the bollock dagger, which had a guard in the form of a pair of lobes and was characteristically worn at the front of the belt like an erect male member. The accounts show that Henry V had at least one example of a short sword or long dagger conventionally worn with civilian dress, the baselard with its H-shaped hilt.

 ## OTHER EDGED WEAPONS

The cavalry lance remained the most popular weapon for use by men-at-arms on horseback. The form of the lance shaft developed in the fourteenth century from a plain staff to one with a narrow grip at the balance point, thickened at the front and rear of this section then tapering to the butt and point. Behind the grip on the tapering butt section was an iron ring or graper; when couched, or gripped securely against the body by the right arm, the butt section rested in the lance rest, an iron or steel bracket attached to the right side of the breastplate. On impact, the backward travel of the lance was stopped by the meeting of the lance rest and graper, imparting the full kinetic energy of horse, rider and armour to the lance point. Judging by artistic representations and later examples, these spears were probably about 10–12 feet (3–3.5 m) in length, though no medieval examples of the hafts survive.

The practice of dismounting to fight on foot by fully armoured knights allowed a range of close combat weapons to be used. Complete armour of plate allowed the knight to dispense with the shield, and to wield weapons in two hands. The most popular weapon for foot combat in England and France was the short lance – not a cut-down version of the cavalry weapon but a short spear, with a head similar in size to the largest crossbow quarrel heads (sometimes called a "dart"). Again, no identifiable medieval examples of these weapons are known to survive, but it is likely that they were similar in form to the spears used for boar hunting, with a haft 5–7 feet (1.5–2 m) in length. The other weapon typical of foot combat by men-at-arms was the pollaxe, a combined axe and hammer head on a haft typically six feet (1.8 m) in length. It was often provided with steel reinforcing bands nailed to the haft and with a steel butt spike so the weapon could be used in a variety of ways – as a short spear, hammer, axe or quarter staff.

Though there is no evidence for its use by English infantry as early as the Agincourt campaign, the hedging bill, a heavy, forward-curved steel blade forged for military use with an additional spike at the front, and fitted with a 5-feet (1.5 m) haft, would become a significant infantry weapon in English service in the mid- and late-fifteenth century. The heavy spiked mace of the Low Countries, the godendag, chandelier or *plançon à picot*, used extensively by the communal forces of the Flemish towns, is occasionally encountered in knightly service in England and France, and evolved in the fifteenth century with the addition of numerous spikes into the "holy water sprinkler".

Other forms of staff weapon were popular with continental infantry, though most of the French pavisiers whose role was to protect crossbowmen while reloading with their large rectangular shields, were armed with conventional spears. Numerous alternative forms of spear with broader, often winged, heads, which could be used for cutting and thrusting, all appear in the early fifteenth century, such as the partisan, *corsèque* and *ronçone*. A form of long-hafted axe, the *voulge*, became very popular among French infantry during the late fourteenth and early fifteenth centuries.

 THE LONGBOW

The longbow, a self bow (one formed of a single stave of wood) of about the same length as the archer's height, though most closely associated with the English armies of the Middle Ages, has a long history in northern Europe. The earliest examples are probably those from bog finds from the Mesolithic in Denmark, dating to about 6000 BC, most of which are made of elm (*ulmus glabra*. Yew (*taxus baccata*) was popular for such bows by about 3300 BC. The earliest known English longbow is the Meare Heath bow, a flat bow of yew dating to about 2500 BC. However, the tradition to which the characteristic English medieval longbow belongs is probably Scandinavian, where mighty bows feature in the sagas. From the time of the Norman Conquest onwards, archers were common, though not numerous, and were not of great tactical importance among medieval English infantry. However, in Wales the use of the longbow appears to have been more widespread. It was in the Welsh wars of Edward I in the late thirteenth century that the longbow was adopted by English archers, not as a new weapon, but as a new tactical use of an ancient one.

The English longbow was formed of a single stave of yew wood, cut so that the pale sapwood formed the outside or back of the bow, and the darker heartwood the inside or belly of the bow. The bows excavated from the *Mary Rose* (1545) show that these bows probably had an average length of 78 inches (6½ feet, just under 2 m), and that their average draw weight, judging by their massive forms, is estimated as ranging between 100 and 180 lb (45–81 kg). They were fitted with horn nocks for the attachment of the bow strings at either end of the stave, but had no fitted grip. Experiments with replicas of these heavy bows show that a particular technique must be learned to shoot them: a single, rolling movement, rather than the draw, hold and loose of modern target archery (which would – even if the archers' bodies could stand it – have been detrimental to the bows themselves). The effect of shooting them over even a relatively short period of time was to cause deformation in the right shoulder and left elbow joints, which can be seen in the skeletons of the archers of the *Mary Rose* and from the mass graves of the Battle of Towton (1461).

Only two types of bow are recorded in the English accounts of the late medieval period. These are the cheaper white bows, which made up the great bulk of the military provision, and painted bows – about twice the price – which were used by members of the royal family and nobility, as well as guards. There seems no distinction between these bows in power or size, just in the quality of their finish. Each bow was supplied with a number of bow strings for service with the English armies in France during the Hundred Years War, a ratio of five bow strings per bow appearing so persistently in the records as to have been a deliberate standard. The bow strings were made of hemp, by a separate guild of longbow string makers who supplied standard strings, not graduated ones designed for different strengths of bows.

 THE ARROW

Arrows were supplied by fletchers, who – for the most part – were centred in London by the late fourteenth century. The arrows were of two main types: broad-heads, exclusively for hunting, and military arrows with a standard form of bullet-shaped head, sharply pointed with a sharp-edged almond-shaped section and with low barbs and a socket at the rear. These were either of iron or "steeled" – made of iron with hardened steel edges and points. The standard type had a shaft of aspen (*populus tremula*, a type of poplar) and was fletched with goose feathers and fitted with iron heads. Millions of these cheaper arrows were made, brought to the Tower of London and issued for campaigns throughout the Hundred Years War. The more expensive type had shafts made of ash wood, were fletched with peacock feathers and had steeled heads.

All arrows were manufactured and distributed in sheaves of 24, tied together with hemp twine. They were carried onto the battlefield using the same twine, tied around the waist and carried at the centre of the back. Quivers are scarcely ever recorded in the accounts and seem not to have been used in a military context. The records of issues throughout the Hundred Years War indicate that most archers were issued with two sheaves of arrows for a campaign and it is likely that they carried only one sheaf of 24 arrows onto the battlefield with them.

 ## THE CROSSBOW

The principal missile weapon of the French army, used by French infantry as well as mercenaries (such as the Genoese who performed so poorly at Crécy), was the crossbow. This weapon had a bow, called a "prod" or "lath", either a self bow of wood or a "horn" bow, a composite bow formed of a combination of horn, wood and sinew to form a very powerful spring, or, by the fifteenth century, bows of steel. A stock or tiller was attached to the bow with a pivoted "nut" to which the bow string could be securely nocked, and released by depressing a lever. The crossbow quarrel was usually one foot (30 cm) in length, of wood (ash where it is specified in the accounts), fletched with hawk feathers and tipped with iron or steeled quarrel heads. Various different spanning techniques were in use simultaneously. Leather baldricks with spanning hooks, used in conjunction with a stirrup at the junction of the bow and tiller, continued to be provided for weapons of lower draw weight. The goat's foot lever, which served as a pivoted fulcrum acting on lugs fitted at either side of the tiller, was probably the most popular spanning system. Newer, heavier crossbows were spanned with windlasses, which provided a much greater mechanical advantage allowing much more powerful bows to be used. However, they were very slow to operate, or used very powerful screw winders, also slow to use.

The ultimate spanning system for the crossbow, the cranequin, which used a rack and pinion mechanism to exert huge mechanical advantage and span the most powerful bows, appeared at the end of the fourteenth century and became popular during the fifteenth. However, ballistic tests on steel crossbows indicate that although they could project heavy quarrels effectively, the velocities achieved and therefore the impact of the missiles were not much greater than those imparted to longbow arrows. Until replaced by handguns (and, in the later fifteenth century in France and Burgundy, longbows), crossbows remained the most important missile weapons in continental western Europe. Their use in fourteenth-century England was much more extensive than is commonly thought, as they were issued in large quantities for the defence of ships and fortifications, as well as being used widely on the noble hunting field. However, there is no evidence of their use on the battlefield by English forces.

 ## FLAGS AND BANNERS

The English army was accompanied throughout the Hundred Years War by a profusion of banners bearing the red cross of St George on a white ground; the same motif appears on lance pennons. The English military ordinances required all members of the army, irrespective of rank, to wear the cross of St George on front and back.

Alongside the banners of St George were others decorated with the arms of the king, usually about one third as numerous, but still in large quantities. The records of the manufacture of banners for the Agincourt campaign fortunately survive in the accounts of Henry V's painter, Robert Tenterdon, and these show a slightly different emphasis from previous reigns. There were 408 banners painted with the arms of St George, alongside 396 bearing the king's arms. Another 140 were painted with the king's arms or his badges, two with the arms of the Holy Trinity, two with St Mary, four with the arms of St Edmund, four with the arms of St Edward and there were other banners for nobles in his army. In addition, there were 5,041 lance pennons newly painted for the campaign, over 3,000 of which bore Henry V's badge, the ostrich feather. That the banners were at Agincourt is attested in the chronicles of Jean Le Fèvre and Jean de Waurin:

> *"Speaking of the banners there was for his own person five banners: the banners of the Trinity, the Virgin, Saint George, Saint Edward and the banner with his own coat of arms on it".*

Another source for Agincourt suggests that the king had with him a banner decorated with his alternative badge of a foxtail.

We are less well endowed with detailed information about the French banners at Agincourt. The French royal arms, blue with three fleurs-de-lys in gold (France modern), were borne ubiquitously after 1376. At about the same time, the French adopted a white cross on a red ground, the arms of the Knights of St John of Jerusalem, and used it in apposition to the English cross of St George. All French soldiers were ordered to wear this white cross.

The most iconic French flag, the *Oriflamme*, the flag of St Denis, was supposed to have been carried on crusade by Charlemagne. Carried at significant French battles from Bouvines (1214) onwards, it was lost at Mons-en-Pévèle, Crécy, Poitiers and, finally, at Agincourt. Its exact appearance is unknown, and it was doubtless replaced several times in the course of its use; it is generally thought to have been a swallow-tailed (or otherwise multi-tailed) banner of silk, plain red or decorated with a sun disc and flames in gold. Mirroring the English use of the banner of St Mary was the adoption by France of the banner of Notre-Dame (our Lady), carried at Nicopolis in 1396.

# 12

# ARMOUR

 ## MAKING ARMOUR

Though plate armour was in existence in the thirteenth century, its use on the battlefield became extensive in the second quarter of the fourteenth century. The mail armour it replaced was not completely discarded, but continued to be worn with complete armours of plate to cover the gaps in armour, at the throat, armpits and groin. Helmet makers had produced defences of iron and steel of solid plate from at least the eleventh century and it was these craftsmen, the helmers, who became the armourers making the newly fashionable plate armour. By the start of the fifteenth century, a typical harness of plate comprised a helmet called a bacinet with a pivoted visor and pendant mail aventail; a "pair of plates", iron plates riveted inside a textile covering which protected the chest, stomach and back; plate arm defences comprising spaudlers for the shoulders, rerebraces for the upper arms, couters for the elbows, vambraces for the lower arms and plate gauntlets; and plate defences for the legs comprising cuisses for the thighs, with poleyns for the knees attached, greaves for the lower legs and sabatons for the feet.

In England, most of this plate armour can be shown, in the few places where we have detailed evidence, to have been imported from abroad. It came mostly from the armour-making centres of north Germany such as Cologne, north Italy and Flanders. Of these, the Milanese armourers were the first to enjoy a reputation as individual craftsmen and to stamp their products, usually in a highly visible location, with their individual makers' marks. There were armourers working in England, but these seem to have been a minority, and not necessarily enjoying the reputation of their continental counterparts. The same is true of mail makers, where fine mail, either or iron wire of the more expensive steel, and all of riveted construction, was imported from Germany or Lombardy in north Italy. In France, the same centres seem to have been used, but there is evidence for a flourishing armour-making industry growing up in Paris during the early fifteenth century.

 ## WHITE ARMOUR

Much, if not most, of the plate armour of the fourteenth century was covered, either in various grades of fabric – from plain fustian to expensive silks, satins and velvets (the latter in a variety of colours, red, blue, green, white and black) – or, less commonly, in leather. Many pieces of armour were made of leather, especially arm and leg defences, though the fashion for these defences appears to have been limited to the middle of the fourteenth century. By the 1370s, most plate armour was made of iron and steel. Defences of mail were also sometimes covered in fabric. However, with the replacement of the fabric-covered pair of plates with the solid-plate breastplate (which began to occur in the early years of the fifteenth century), there came a new fashion for "white" armour, that is, uncovered armour of polished metal.

Manuscript accounts of the period show that the old and new styles were being worn together, though much of the artistic evidence suggests that everyone was wearing the new fashion. It is difficult to be sure how this bright polished armour was finished, that is, whether the exterior was polished bright steel or blackened. The blackened finish was created either by retaining and polishing the coating of dark iron oxide on the surface of the worked steel, or by chemically blackening the surface. Certainly, the fashion in northern Europe by the middle of the fifteenth century was for blackened armour and this fashion persisted until the end of the seventeenth century; it can be seen in countless paintings, though the fashion for polishing armour bright in the nineteenth century removed many of the original finishes which had remained on surviving pieces of armour.

From the late fourteenth century, the new-style uncovered armour was decorated with applied borders of bands of latten, usually themselves decorated with engraved ornament. Helmets had always been decorated; the great helms of the thirteenth and early fourteenth centuries had been fitted with elaborate heraldic crests and those of royalty with silver-gilt crowns. This fashion lasted into the early fifteenth century and the surviving bacinet of Charles V or VI from Chartres Cathedral originally bore such a crown riveted onto the skull, along with a complex pendant ornament of silver gilt chains and enamel panels.

 HELMETS

Alongside the change to white armour came a development in the helmets worn by knights on the battlefield. The great helm had long ago been relegated to the tournament. Although it was ideal protection in single combat on horseback in the joust, it was useless for fighting on foot. The great helm was replaced in the middle of the fourteenth century by the bacinet, a helmet with a skull fitting the top and rear of the head, and provided with a mail aventail covering the nape of the neck and throat and extending over the shoulders, which provided a flexible defence. This had been worn under the great helm in the early fourteenth century, but with the change of fashion for men-at-arms towards fighting on foot rather than on horseback – which happened across much of northern and western Europe around the middle of the fourteenth century – the bacinet became the principal head defence worn on the battlefield. Crucially, it provided the knight with peripheral vision, essential for fighting on foot. It was rapidly furnished with a face defence of its own, either one pivoted at the centre of the forehead, known by the German term *Klappvisier*, or with a visor pivoted at either temple.

By the early fifteenth century, the bacinet was replaced by the "great bacinet", in which the mail aventail was replaced by solid plate defences for the nape of the neck and for the throat, and the two types of bacinet were probably worn by the vast majority of men-at-arms on either side at Agincourt. Another form of helmet that had evolved in the thirteenth century, the wide-brimmed kettle hat, which provided a good balance of vision and protection, remained popular throughout the fourteenth and fifteenth centuries.

 ## THE EFFECTIVENESS OF PLATE ARMOUR

In the 1330s, the transition of battlefield armour from mail to plate occurred so rapidly and pervasively across Europe (creating the very image of the medieval knight encased in steel) that scholars have sought to explain it. Some have suggested that it was brought about by a technological change, that the ability to work large enough sheets of iron and steel enabled armourers to make pieces of plate armour. But helms had been made before plate armour became popular, and much of the plate armour was made in any case out of relatively small plates articulated together. Other scholars have suggested that warfare simply became more violent, that weapon strokes became heavier, but this seems improbable. Some have blamed the longbow: the transition happened at exactly the same time that the English system of longbowmen fighting alongside dismounted men-at-arms came into prominence. Yet the transition happened across Europe, including in areas where the longbow was scarcely of importance as a distance weapon. Others have suggested that the improvement in crossbow technology was behind the change, since it happened at the same time as new spanning techniques. The windlass, gaffle (or goat's foot lever) and cranequin enabled crossbow makers to fit more and more powerful bows that could, in turn, shoot heavier quarrels faster; these are found across the whole of Europe in exactly the same areas as plate armour.

Ballistic testing shows that the longbow was able to deliver similar velocities to its arrows as a crossbow could to its quarrels. The bodkin arrowhead, often described as a plate armour-piercing head, appears mostly in thirteenth-century contexts before the widespread adoption of plate armour. The arrow heads most closely associated with the fourteenth and early fifteenth centuries are a quite different form – the "type 16" head, with a sharp, barbed almond-shaped head attached to the socket.

The difficulty of accurately testing the effectiveness of these weapons against armour are many: today we have no archers trained to shoot the longbow from boyhood and we have not a single surviving example of a medieval English longbow to replicate. The cache of bows from the *Mary Rose*, Henry VIII's great warship, which sank in the Solent in 1545, remains the closest we have to the medieval war bow. Precious little medieval armour from the period of Agincourt or earlier survives, though we have enough knowledge to reconstruct with a fair degree of accuracy the armour of the time of the battle. The difficulty of testing the effectiveness of the longbow lies partly with finding archers accurate enough with the weapon to simulate the archery of the English armies of the Hundred Years War. This has led investigators to use either mathematics to assess the impact of arrows on their targets or other forms of propulsion in a laboratory, in either case to simulate a theoretical rather than actual performance with a bow in a field. It is these tests that have led to the idea of the invincible penetrating power of the arrow shot from the longbow. Older tests carried out in more lifelike conditions have shown that plate armour in excess of 1mm in thickness is generally impermeable to arrows from longbows or crossbow quarrels unless struck at 90 degrees and 2mm steel to be impermeable at any angle.

 ## ARMOURED HORSES

Throughout the fourteenth and fifteenth centuries, some warhorses were equipped with armour, though probably never as many as artistic representations suggest. More of them were provided with textile trappers, which provided a heraldic function in helping to identify their riders as well as providing limited protection for the horse.

The earliest type of medieval European horse armour was the trapper or bard of mail. Examples of these appear in art throughout the thirteenth and fourteenth centuries, as well as being recorded in the accounts of the time. Such armours were probably redundant by the early fifteenth century, though manuscript illustrations continue to depict mail elements of horse armour, especially for neck defences or crinets.

By the middle of the fourteenth century, plate head defences of iron or steel for horses, known as shaffrons, were being used alongside mail bards. In the middle of the fourteenth century, hardened leather horse armours became popular, with leather plate shaffrons used alongside defences for the front of the horse (the peytral), the flanks (flanchards) and rear (crupper). Like plate armour for the knight, such leather bards appear to have become restricted to the tournament arena by the early fifteenth century.

At about this time, iron versions of the leather defences, especially peytrals and crinets, appear in artistic representations, but they are not recorded in the financial accounts and probably had a limited currency. The Tower armoury accounts of the fourteenth century give an indication of just how little horse armour was used in England at that time. We do not have comparable sources for France, but documentary evidence suggests that more horse armour was used there. Mounted men-at-arms at the Battle of Poitiers of 1356, for example, clearly indicate the French knights' belief in the defensive qualities of their horse armour against English arrows, and the French mounted charges at Agincourt are probably part of the same tradition.

Surviving examples of horse armour of the period are extremely limited. However, the celebrated Warwick shaffron, heirloom of the earls at Warwick Castle and now part of the national collection of the Royal Armouries, may have been worn by the horse of Richard Beauchamp, Earl of Warwick (d. 1439) in the early fifteenth century. Beauchamp was captain of Calais in 1415 and does not appear to have been present at the Battle of Agincourt.

 EQUIPPING THE ROYAL HOUSEHOLD

Throughout the fourteenth century, the kings of England had armourers in their households. Some of these, such as John of Cologne, Edward III's armourer, were not really armourers in the modern sense at all but rather tailors and embroiderers (or "linen armourers"). Plate armour was made until the middle of the fourteenth century by helmers or helm makers, men skilled in shaping and riveting plates of iron and steel. In 1375, at the death of Edward's last helmer, William Swynley, his workshop at the Tower was transferred to William Snell, the king's armourer. Snell served until 1395, when he retired with a monetary grant for life after 36 years' service owing to his "old age and feebleness".

Armourers working for Henry IV include Stephen atte Frith, Giles Fox and John Dounton, who in turn were replaced as armourers of the king's body by John Hill in 1408. Hill was replaced by Martin Pull in 1413, but Pull died in 1415 and Hill was reinstated. Hill is interesting as the only armourer known to have written a manual – on the subject of foot combat. All these men made plate armour for Henry IV and his son Prince Henry, including bacinets, pairs of plate alongside the new-style breastplates, complete armours of plate as well as brigandines. These were in such quantities as to be clearly for distribution, probably as gifts – if the pattern established by Edward III was continued – to members of the royal family and nobility, and not solely for the king's personal use.

 THE ARMOUR OF THE ORDINARY SOLDIER

Though the equipment of shire archers raised by commissions of array for service in England was minimal, that of the mounted archers who fought at Agincourt was probably fairly extensive. Throughout the second half of the fourteenth century, the Tower armoury had kept a great stock of mail shirts (habergeons), bacinets lacking visors but with aventails, and kettle hats for issue to English archers. From the 1370s onwards, these were supplemented by the quilted jack (precursor of the Tudor "jack of plate"), and a form of head defence called a palet, probably a skull cap worn without an aventail.

The brigandine, a form of body armour that evolved from the pair of plates, with, as the fifteenth century progressed, smaller plates riveted inside the textile covering, appears in the accounts at the end of the fourteenth century. By the middle of the fifteenth century, it became the standard type of body armour for the well equipped mounted archer of English retinues. English archers were also equipped with horn bucklers – small, round shields – for which there are extensive records in the Tower. Pavises (large standing shields) were also made in substantial quantities in England and were often issued for use on ships. There is no evidence that they were used by English longbowmen in battle, but they were used extensively by French crossbowmen and infantry spearmen called "pavisiers" after their shields.

# 13

# ARTILLERY

 ## NON-GUNPOWDER ARTILLERY

Since Roman times, a variety of siege weapons had been in use in western Europe. These included stone-throwing engines, such as trebuchets and bolt shooting engines, such as springalds. The former type comprised large machines constructed out of large quantities of materials including wood, iron and rope. These were powered by using counter-weights to draw back the arms of these stone throwers or alternatively they were pulled back manually using ropes. Some of these weapons were even given their own names, such as the *Warwolf*, constructed for Edward I during the siege of Berwick-upon-Tweed in 1304. Stone throwers were regularly employed at sieges during the Hundred Years War, including at Harfleur in 1415.

The other commonly used type of artillery was the springald, a type of large crossbow firing large quarrels or bolts, which drew its power from the tension caused by drawing back on its string. They were regularly mentioned in inventories in the late fourteenth and early fifteenth centuries, such as for the arsenal at the Tower of London and at Calais. Traditional artillery continued to be used throughout the fifteenth century, but it increasingly began to be supplanted by the new technology of gunpowder weapons.

A NEW TECHNOLOGY FROM THE EAST

Gunpowder weapons originated in China and had reached western Europe by the early fourteenth century. Some knowledge of gunpowder itself, however, appears to have arrived earlier in the thirteenth century, as the English alchemist and philosopher Roger Bacon, referred to a gunpowder-like substance in his works *The Epistolae*, *Opus Majus* and *Opus Tertium*. The earliest discovered reference to a gun in an English source occurs in a document presented to Edward III on his accession to the throne in 1327. This consisted of a treatise on kingship, which provided guidance on how to be a good ruler. It also includes an image of a cauldron-shaped gun lying on a trestle that is firing a bolt or arrow from its muzzle. The new technology took some time to be developed during the reign of Edward III, although gunpowder demonstrations were staged as early as 1334. According to Italian accounts, the English used guns at the Battle of Crécy in 1346, which helped to disrupt the French attacks. Later the same year, 10 guns were transported from the royal arsenal at the Tower of London to France for the siege of Calais (which surrendered in August 1347). However these weapons had little effect on the ultimate outcome, in part due to their small size and the high price of gunpowder.

Further changes occurred in the late fourteenth century, however, which meant that much larger guns began to be used. This can be seen with the siege of the English-held Saint-Sauveur-le-Vicomte (1374–75); the large French guns caused significant damage to the defences of the town, which led to its surrender. Guns also began to be used for furnishing castles. The earliest record of this in England occurred in 1365, when two large guns and nine smaller guns were sent to the king's new castle of Queenborough on the Isle of Sheppey. Later in the reign of Richard II, large numbers of guns were sent to royal castles during the great invasion scare of 1385–86, when the French attempted to invade England on two occasions. By the end of the fourteenth century, guns were still used alongside traditional artillery, but they were becoming increasingly useful in siege warfare.

 CREATING GUNPOWDER

Gunpowder, also known as "Black Powder", is made from three components, saltpetre (potassium nitrate), sulphur and charcoal. The optimum ratio of these ingredients was eventually established at 75 per cent saltpetre, 10 per cent sulphur and 15 per cent charcoal. Originally, these were mixed together using a pestle and mortar, in much the same way that a cake is prepared in a mixing bowl. Once set on fire, gunpowder becomes an incendiary as opposed to explosive substance (it does not react quickly enough to qualify as the latter). Its destructive properties meant that gunpowder was first used for incendiary bombs and later for firing projectiles through metal guns by the Chinese.

One of the most fundamental barriers to the development of gunpowder weapons in the fourteenth century was the high price of gunpowder. This essentially was due to the low availability and high cost of the most important ingredient, saltpetre. England was entirely dependent on imports of saltpetre prior to the sixteenth century. For much of the fourteenth century, this substance was imported from as far afield as India, via Italian merchants. The development of saltpetre plantations in continental northern Europe in the late fourteenth century, however, led to a significant decrease in prices.

By contrast, the other ingredients for gunpowder were easier to obtain, with sulphur imported from southern Italy and with charcoal readily available from native English trees. This meant that by the reign of Henry V, gunpowder was available in larger quantities and at a lower price (typically 6d a pound). He was therefore able to make extensive use of gunpowder artillery in his siege of Harfleur in 1415 and in the conquest of Normandy in 1417–19. Later in the fifteenth century, gunpowder was made specifically for different types of guns, with very fine, fast-burning gunpowder for small weapons, such as handguns, and much coarser gunpowder for larger weapons, such as bombards.

## THE TOWER OF LONDON AND THE PRODUCTION OF GUNS

By 1415, the Tower of London had long been an important centre for the production and storage of artillery. Since the reign of Edward III, the department of the Privy Wardrobe had been responsible for the provision of weaponry for the furnishing of royal armies and garrisons. This was located in the Tower and was administered by an official known as the Keeper of the Privy Wardrobe. Further work for the 1415 expedition was undertaken by a German gunner called Gerard Sprong, recruited during the reign of Henry IV, and by the metal founder and citizen of London, William Woodward. In this period, guns were either forged out of wrought iron metal by gunners or smith, or alternatively they were made out of cast bronze by bell founders. The majority of the guns, particularly the larger ones, fired stones carved by masons, whereas the smaller guns fired lead shot. They were not provided with their own individual wooden carriages; instead they were transported in large carts pulled by oxen or horses. If they were to be used offensively in a siege, the guns would then be taken out of their carts once they had reached their destination and mounted on wooden beds (a process referred to as "stocking") prior to being fired.

Henry was keen to invade France with as impressive an artillery train as could possibly be assembled, as can be seen with the extensive efforts made to construct guns for the expedition. On 12 February 1414, the king's smith, William atte Mersh, was appointed to take smiths for making certain guns of the king and for ironwork ordered within the Tower of London, as well as for the carriage of iron, coal and other items. Six days later, the merchant, John Stevens, was paid over £100 towards the construction of a large gun at Bristol. A Master William

Gunmaker was then paid over £40 for the purchase of 18,000 lb (8,165 kg) of iron for the construction of guns in July of the same year. Later in December, a commission was given to William Woodward and Gerard Sprong to take all manner of iron, bronze and other things from London and elsewhere, including the king's kitchen, for the production of guns.

A full inventory of the guns transported to France in 1415 does not survive; however, a set of accounts submitted by Gerard Sprong reveals some of the artillery available to Henry in the same year. This included five large named guns called *Clysf*, *Fowler*, *Bristol*, *George*, and *God's Grace*, in addition to other equipment, such as horse harnesses, gunstones and a pair of bellows. Some idea of the munitions supplied for the expedition can also be seen with the 10,000 gunstones purchased in October 1414. This meant that Henry V's expedition to France was the best-equipped English army to date for artillery.

 GUNS IN ACTION

English guns began to play a more important offensive role in siege warfare during the reign of Henry IV. At the end of May 1405, Gerard Sprong was instructed by Henry IV to take guns from the Tower of London for an expedition to the north to quell a rebellion by the Earl of Northumberland. The artillery was then subsequently used at the sieges of Warkworth and Berwick castles with at least 950 lb (430 kg) of gunpowder expended. According to Hardyng's chronicle, the garrison of the former surrendered after just seven shots were fired at it. Henry while Prince of Wales gained experience of using guns in warfare during the Owain Glyndŵr rebellion, particularly in the sieges of Aberystwyth and Harlech castles, with 2,825 lb (1,281 kg) of gunpowder expended at the latter. Henry V's experience of siege warfare in Wales is likely to have played a part in his desire to have an impressive artillery train for the invasion of France.

The requirements of operating and maintaining a large number of gunners meant that a large ordnance company had to be assembled. In addition to the 78 gunners recruited for the expedition, a support company of 100 masons, 120 carpenters, 30 smiths and 60 carters were also hired, as well as large numbers of labourers. Accounts of the siege, such as in *Gesta Henrici Quinti*, make it clear that the English guns played an important role in encouraging the garrison to surrender. These were deployed around the perimeter of the town, protected from the French guns and other missile weapons by large wooden structures called mantlets, which were erected by carpenters. The defenders were said to be "sorely troubled by the scourge of the stones and almost despairing of being rescued by the French", which led to their decision to surrender the town. Such was the damage caused to the town by the English that they themselves subsequently had difficulties defending the settlement. This can be seen by the financial accounts of the treasurer of Harfleur for 1415–20, which lists numerous repairs carried out to the walls and other defences. After the capture of the town, artillery played no further part in the 1415 campaign, as the gunners and guns were left behind at Harfleur. Guns did play an important role in Henry's second expedition to France, in 1417, particularly at the siege of Caen.

Gunpowder weapons were also used in small numbers on royal warships in the reign of Henry V. Out of 16 royal warships in 1416, only four were armed with guns, with four guns on the *Thomas of the Tower*, three guns on the *Grand Mary of the Tower*, one on the Katherine of the Tower and one on the *Red Cog of the Tower*. However, these only played a very limited role in naval warfare during this period.

# THE RELIABILITY OF GUNS

Early gunpowder weapons have a modern reputation for being unreliable and potentially dangerous to their own side. Perhaps the best known example of a gun misfiring from the period is the Flemish gun the Lion, which broke during the siege of Roxburgh Castle in 1460. On 3 August, King James II of Scotland, while standing next to the gun when it was fired, was mortally wounded as a result of a fragment of the stock breaking and shattering his thigh bone in two. Guns certainly did break under the strain of firing in the fifteenth century on a regular basis. When Henry V, as Prince of Wales, besieged the rebel-held Aberystwyth Castle, at least four of his guns broke, including the Messenger which was made out of bronze and weighed 4,800lbs. Guns were, however, an effective weapon of war in the fifteenth century that were widely used in siege warfare. As demonstrated by Henry V, they could be effective in damaging fortifications and, therefore, decreasing the length of time it took to capture enemy settlements. They could also, on occasion, be useful in killing enemy personnel: in the reign of Henry's son and successor, Henry VI, Thomas Montague, Earl of Salisbury, was mortally wounded as a result of enemy gunfire at the siege of Orléans in 1428.

# A REVOLUTIONARY TECHNOLOGY

After Henry V's death, in 1422, artillery played a crucial role in the war against the supporters of the dauphin (who was later crowned Charles VII). Expeditions sent to France in the reign of Henry VI were furnished with large quantities of gunpowder weapons, such as with the army that besieged Orléans in 1428. Guns were later to be used with great success against the English by the French in their re-conquest of Normandy in 1449–50 and Aquitaine in 1451. Two years later, at the Battle of Castillon, an English army led by John Talbot, which had tried to regain Aquitaine, was decisively defeated – this was in large part due to French artillery.

Significant changes occurred to guns during the second half of the fifteenth century, which evolved into a large variety of different types. Artillery was used regularly on the battlefield, such as during the battles of the Wars of the Roses in England. Guns also came to play an increasingly important role in naval warfare. These changes continued into the sixteenth century. By the death of Henry VIII, in 1547, huge resources were devoted to the production, use and storage of artillery. This can be seen by the inventories compiled during the reign of his son, Edward VI, which detail many thousands of guns scattered across a large number of town and fortifications, as well as from the wreck of the *Mary Rose* (which sank in 1545 and was lifted from the Solent in 1982), which bristled with a variety of heavy iron and bronze guns. Over time, this technology supplanted traditional weapons such as the longbow, whose usage had largely died out by the end of the sixteenth century.

# 14

# THE LEGACY OF AGINCOURT

 THE V-SIGN

It is often claimed that English success at Agincourt is the origin of a rude hand gesture known as the "V-sign". In this gesture, the second and third fingers form a V-shape and are displayed with the back of the hand towards the person to be insulted. The story goes that before the battle, the French, supremely confident they were going to win, had threatened to cut off those very same fingers of any English archer they captured. Afterwards, the English gloated in their victory by showing the French in no uncertain terms that they still had their fingers.

It is a great tale but no one has been able to discover when it was first put forward. No chronicle account of the battle has the archers making any gesture to the French after the victory, nor is there any evidence in this period that if archers were captured in any engagement, they had their fingers cut off by their captors.

However, in chronicle accounts of the battle, there are two interesting references to possible mutilation. Thomas Walsingham says that the French had announced before the battle that they would spare no one save for the king and his leading lords. The rest would be killed or would have their limbs horribly mutilated. In the pre-battle speech put into Henry's mouth by the Burgundian chroniclers Jean Le Fèvre and Jean de Waurin, the king allegedly told his troops that the French had boasted that if any English archers were captured "they would cut off three fingers of their right hand so that neither man or horse would ever again be killed by their arrow shot". Possibly someone in a later century read this and imagined the invention of the V-sign as a result. The idea of Agincourt as the origin of the gesture has no doubt been stimulated by the love–hate relationship that exists between the British and their French neighbours. The gesture has also come to represent a snub towards authority and the establishment.

## EARLY BATTLEFIELD TOURISM (EDWARD IV)

In 1475, King Edward IV visited the site of the Battle of Agincourt fought 60 years earlier. The evidence for this comes from a letter written by a John Albon to Thomas Palmer, esquire, of Holt in Leicestershire. It is recorded that Edward and his lords, including the king's friend and chamberlain William, Lord Hastings, were at the battle site on 27 July. Three days earlier, a group of French captains had been at Agincourt. Albon was optimistic that some of them would transfer their allegiance to the English king.

In 1460–61, the Yorkists had overthrown Henry VI, whose father, Henry V, had defeated the French at Agincourt in 1415. With the help of the French king, Louis XI, Henry VI had been put back on the English throne in 1470, forcing Edward IV to take exile in the Low Countries. After his restoration in 1471 (which led to the murder of Henry VI), Edward was keen to renew the war with France. In 1475, he led an army of over 11,000 men, close to the size of Henry V's expeditionary army in 1415, to France. The letter tells us that Edward was keen to give battle. But this time there was no fight. The French king, mindful of how dangerous battles could be, bought Edward off.

# ⚜ COMMEMORATING THE BATTLE (HENRY VIII)

In a text written in the 1530s or 40s, Henry VIII was urged to stage annual triumphs as anti-papal propaganda. One of the examples of good practice that the author mentioned was the yearly celebration at Calais of the English victory at Agincourt:

> *"For the victory that God gave to your most valiant predecessor, King Henry the Fifth, with so little a number of his countrymen against so great a multitude of the Frenchmen at the Battle of Agincourt, your retinue at your noble town of Calais, and others over there, yearly make a solemn triumph, going in procession, lauding God, shooting guns, with the noise and melody of trumpets and other instruments, to the great rejoicing of your subjects who are aged, the comfort of those who are able, and the encouraging of young children."*

Calais was the only English continental possession that remained at the end of the Hundred Years War, having been originally captured by Edward III in 1347. Its location, in the Straits of Dover, meant that English armies could be easily transported to and from mainland Europe. In 1513, Henry VIII had invaded France with a large army and defeated the French at the Battle of the Spurs. He failed to emulate the achievements of his ancestor Henry V, however, and came to terms with King Louis XII of France. Calais was later captured by a French army led by Francis, Duke of Guise, in 1558.

# SHAKESPEARE AND AGINCOURT

Shakespeare's famous play *Henry V* (1599) has shaped views of the Battle of Agincourt, as well as the king more generally. The drama is very much focused on preparations for the invasion of France, the battle and its aftermath. It skews history in moving straight from the victory to the Treaty of Troyes. In reality, Henry's conquest of Normandy between 1417 and 1419, and the assassination of John the Fearless, Duke of Burgundy in September 1419 at the behest of the dauphin and the Armagnac faction, were the key events in making it possible for Henry to be accepted by the French as heir to the throne and regent.

The actual battle scenes in Shakespeare's play (Act 4, scenes 4–6) contain very little dialogue. Its first vignette is Pistol's capture of a Frenchman, which allows for a comic dialogue based on a misunderstanding of French. This is followed by an exchange between the Constable of France and the Dukes of Bourbon and Orléans during which they realize the French are being defeated. In the last of the three scenes, Henry has an exchange with the Duke of Exeter (a peer who was not actually at the battle), who comes to tell the king of the death of the Duke of York. The first scene of the three is headed with the stage prompt, "Alarms and Excursions". "Alarms" would have taken the form of drum rolls and perhaps trumpets. "Excursions" were characters running on and off, and across the stage, but there may also have been some hand-to-hand combat using stage swords. Intriguingly, there are no archers in Shakespeare's *Henry V*.

# WATERLOO AND AGINCOURT

A description of the site of the battlefield from the early nineteenth century survives from John Gordon Smith (1792–1833). A Scottish surgeon, he was attached to the 12th Lancers and had served at the Battle of Waterloo in 1815, the great victory of the British and their allies against the French.

Smith was one of the soldiers rewarded for his service at Waterloo by being awarded a medal at Agincourt on 17 May 1816 (the place was chosen to invoke the link with past successes). He reminisced on this event in a paper read before the Royal Society of Literature on 4 April 1827. He was clearly aware of the reputation of the battle fought 400 years previously, which he described as "the scarcely less glorious triumph of Harry the Fifth of England". In 1816, Smith had been stationed with part of the British Army near to the site of the battlefield. He was not particularly impressed with the area, which he described as "consisting of a most un-interesting collection of farmers' residences and cottages'. Nevertheless, Smith believed that he had identified the location of the wood where "the King concealed those archers whose prowess and valour contributed so eminently to the glorious result."

 EXCAVATIONS AT AGINCOURT

Excavations at the site of the Battle of Agincourt were undertaken in the spring of 1818. They were carried out by John Woodford, quartermaster-general in the Army of Observation in the Pas de Calais from the aftermath of Waterloo to October 1818. Woodford (1785–1879), had served in the British army at the Battle of Waterloo in 1815, where he had acted as an aide-de-camp to Wellington at headquarters, and had a distinguished military career, reaching the rank of Lieutenant Colonel and being knighted.

Woodford wrote to his brother telling him of the excavations and of his finds. A report written in *The Calendonian Mercury*, dated 25 May 1818, states that a number of items were recovered from the battlefield, including gold coins, lance-heads, rings and arrowheads. Woodford's letters also speak of human remains, and it has been assumed that his excavations had focused on the believed site of the French grave pits. His excavations were cut short by local protests. Finds from his excavations were taken back to England, but appear to have been destroyed by a fire at the Pantechnicon in Belgrave Square, London, in 1874.

A plan that Woodford drew of the battlefield in 1818 still survives at the British Library in London: he placed the position of the French grave pits on the Tramecourt side of the battlefield. Recent archaeological work by Dr Tim Sutherland has failed to locate exactly where Woodford excavated or to find any grave pits, but the search goes on. At present there is no object that can be shown to come from the battlefield.

 ## THE CENTRE HISTORIQUE MÉDIÉVAL AT AGINCOURT

Today's visitor to the battlefield should not miss the Centre Historique Médiéval in the village of Agincourt (modern-day Azincourt). Opened in 2001, the centre was extended in 2005–06 to provide additional education facilities and a multi-purpose medieval-style barn. The first building has a very distinctive and evocative façade, being made to resemble six longbows with arrows about to be loosened. The architects were Eric Revet and Bertrand Klein. Inside, there is a small model of the battlefield as well as audio-visual displays and replica weapons and armour. Visitors can gain a good impression of how heavy some of the weapons were. There are plans for a refurbishment of the centre in 2016.

 ## MEMORIALS

Around 40 brasses and tomb chests survive of Englishmen present on the Agincourt campaign, although in some cases these were men invalided home from Harfleur who did not get to fight at the battle. A good example is Henry V's eldest brother, Thomas, Duke of Clarence, who was sent home sick. After his death on

22 March 1421 at the Battle of Baugé – a French victory – his body was brought back for burial in Canterbury Cathedral. Initially it was placed close to the tomb of his father, Henry IV, in the Trinity Chapel near to the shrine of Thomas Becket. By 1440, a splendid tomb was made for him in St Michael's chapel in the south-west transept of the cathedral, although the duke's effigy is found not only alongside his wife Margaret Holland but also her first husband, John Beaufort, Marquess of Somerset. Henry V's own tomb in Westminster Abbey has above it a chantry chapel with carvings in stone of the king at his crowning as well as on horseback in the field. This may be an allusion to his military successes but there is nothing to indicate that the intention was to portray him at Agincourt.

In England and France no tomb makes an allusion to the battle at all. This is not surprising as it was not common on medieval inscriptions to say much about a person's career. The brass of Sir John Phelip in St Mary's Church, Kidderminster, however, notes his death at the siege of Harfleur.

At the battlefield itself, a *calvaire* was erected after the Franco-Prussian War of 1870 close to where it is traditionally believed the grave pits of the French dead of Agincourt lay. This invoked continuity between those who had fallen in 1415 and more recently. But the first dedicated monument to the battle was not erected until 1963. This simple stone pillar lies on the southern edge of the battlefield and is marked "Azincourt 1415". Subsequently, it has been surrounded by smaller memorials, including one to Le Gallois de Fougières, the provost-marshal who died at the battle. The office he held later evolved into the modern Gendarmerie in France. His remains, buried after the battle in the church of Auchy-lès-Hesdin, were exhumed in the 1930s and are now at the Gendarmerie monument at Versailles.

# THE 600ᵀᴴ ANNIVERSARY OF AGINCOURT

In both France and England, there are commemorations planned for the 600th anniversary of the battle. There has been particular interest from the City of London and its livery companies, which have formed the backbone of the Agincourt 600 committee. The city made a generous loan to Henry V to support his campaign. The enthusiasm of the livery companies, especially the warrior companies such as the Bowyers, Fletchers, Armourers and Brasiers, Cutlers and Gunmakers, stems from the role their ancestors played in producing arms and armour of the kind which might well have found itself used on the campaign. A special float is planned for the 2015 Lord Mayor's Show, for instance, as well as a banquet at the Guildhall.

The "joyous news" of the victory reached London on 29 October 1415. It is wholly appropriate, therefore, that there should be a service of commemoration at Westminster Abbey on 29 October 2015 in which the City of London and its livery companies as well as others who wish to share in the commemoration will take part.

2015 is a year of many anniversaries. In his Budget statement on 18 March, the Chancellor of the Exchequer, George Osborne, announced the allocation of a million pounds to commemorate the 200th anniversary of Waterloo and the 600th anniversary of Agincourt. The chancellor took advantage of his mention of Agincourt to make a modern political jibe about both Europe and Scottish independence: he told MPs that the battle was a manifestation of a strong leader defeating "an ill-judged alliance between the champion of a united Europe and a renegade force of Scottish nationalism", joking that it would be well worth the million pounds to celebrate this special historical moment. He was being a little careless with the truth. Although there was still a Franco–Scottish alliance in place in 1415 (the Auld Alliance first begun in the face of Edward I's attacks on Scotland in the mid-1290s) and Scottish troops were found in French armies in the 1420s, no

Scottish soldiers are believed to have been present on the French side at Agincourt. There was, however, one Welshman, Henry Gwyn, who is known to have fought and died for the French in the battle.

Agincourt 600 Wales has also organized many commemorative events, including a touring exhibition in South Wales, linked to the company of archers recruited in that area in 1415. Elsewhere in England, events of different kinds are being staged, such as those at Erpingham in Norfolk, the seat of Sir Thomas Erpingham who played a command role at the battle. His kneeling effigy, in the extremely fashionable design of the early fifteenth century, was once close to the high altar in Norwich Cathedral. It now tops the gate into the Cathedral Close. Both Norwich Cathedral and St Albans Cathedral, the burial place of Henry V's youngest brother, Humphrey, Duke of Gloucester (who was wounded at the battle), will be staging commemorative events.

A Royal Armouries exhibition about Agincourt, with splendid objects on show and the first scale-model of the battle to be created, is being staged on the top floor of the White Tower in the Tower of London. At the Musée de l'Armée in Paris there is also an exhibition tracing the development of the French army and especially artillery between the defeat at Agincourt and the victory at Marignan in 1515. In Southampton, the main point of embarkation for the expedition, there are many events, including a play about the plot to take Henry's life as he prepared to set sail.

In France the focus of activities is the battlefield itself. The Centre Historique Médiéval is staging its customary re-enactment in late July with an arrow shower involving several hundred archers. At the actual anniversary on 25 October there will be a special event, invoking not only the 600th anniversary but also the 500th in 1915, when French troops invited the British to join them "on the scene of the battle and commemorate the day in unison". As commentators noted, "this joint celebration of an ancient battle-day of honourable memory to both" was testimony to the close alliance between the two nations, now united against a common enemy.

# FURTHER READING

The most thorough general history of the Hundred Years War is given in Jonathan Sumption's series of books, published by Faber: volume 1, *Trial by Battle (1990)*, volume 2, *Trial by Fire* (1999), volume 3, *Divided Houses* (2009) and volume 4, *Cursed Kings (2015)*, which together cover the period from the early fourteenth century to 1422. A final volume on the last stage of the war to 1453 is forthcoming. For useful single volume accounts, see Christopher Allmand, *The Hundred Years War* (Cambridge University Press, 1988) and Anne Curry, *The Hundred Years War* (Palgrave Macmillan, 2nd edn, 2003). A stimulating discussion of the origins of the war is to be found in Malcolm Vale, *The Angevin Legacy and the Hundred Years War 1250–1340* (Blackwell, 1990).

War with France in the reign of Edward III is studied in detail in Clifford Rogers' two books, published by the Boydell Press, *The Wars of Edward III* (1999) and *War Cruel and Sharp. English Strategy under Edward III, 1327–1360* (2000), with the most extensive study of the Battle of Crécy by Andrew Ayton and Philip Preston, *The Battle of Crécy 1346* (Boydell Press, 2005). The best biography of the Black Prince is Richard Barber's *Edward, Prince of Wales and Aquitaine, A Biography of the Black Prince* (Boydell Press, 2003). Peter Hoskins' *In the Steps of the Black Prince, The Road to Poitiers 1355–1356 (Boydell Press, 2012)* gives a full account of the Black Prince's expedition leading to his great victory at Poitiers. For Edward III as king and warrior, see Mark Ormrod, *Edward III* (Yale University Press, 2012).

For the reign of Henry V as a whole, see Christopher Allmand, *Henry V* (Methuen, 1992, now in the Yale Monarchs series), John Matusiak, *Henry V* (Routledge, 2013) and Anne Curry, *Henry V* (Penguin Monarchs, Allen Lane, 2015). On Agincourt, see Juliet Barker, *Agincourt. The King, the Campaign and the Battle* (Little Brown, 2005) and Anne Curry, *Agincourt. A New History* (Tempus, 2005; 2nd edn, The History Press, 2015). Anne Curry has also provided a full guide to sources, with many translated extracts, in *The Battle of Agincourt. Sources and Interpretations* (Boydell, 2000, now available as an e-book). Curry's *Great Battles. Agincourt* (Oxford University Press, 2015) considers the legacy of the battle from the fifteenth century to the present day, as does Stephen Cooper's *Agincourt: Myth and Reality 1415–2015* (Pen and Sword, 2014). *Agincourt 1415: A Tourist's Guide to the Campaign* (Pen and Sword, 2014) by Peter Hoskins (with Anne Curry) tells the story of the Agincourt campaign and guides the tourist along Henry V's itinerary from his landing near Harfleur through to the battlefield and on to Calais.

For the later stages of the Hundred Years War, Juliet Barker provides a full account in *Conquest: The English Kingdom of France 1417–1450* (Little Brown, 2009), with further detail in Ralph Griffiths, *The Reign of Henry VI: the Exercise of Royal Authority, 1422–1461* (Benn, 1981). Helen Castor, *Joan of Arc* (Faber, 2014) and Kelly de Vries, *Joan of Arc: A Military Leader* (Sutton Publishing, 2003) together provide insights into this fascinating woman who turned the tide of the war in the favour of the French.

The best introduction to English armies in the Middle Ages is by Michael Prestwich, *Armies and Warfare in the Middle Ages: the English Experience* (Yale University Press, 1996). For the armies of the fourteenth century, see also Andrew Ayton, *Knights and Warhorses; Military Service and the English Aristocracy under Edward III* (Boydell Press, 1994) and Adrian Bell, *War and the Soldier in the Fourteenth Century* (Boydell Press, 2004), and for the later middle ages as a whole, Adrian Bell, Anne Curry,

Andy King and David Simpkin, *The Soldier in Later Medieval England* (Oxford University Press, 2013). For European medieval warfare in general, see Philippe Contamine, *War in the Middle Ages* (Blackwell, 1984). Also useful is Anne Curry and Michael Hughes, *Arms, Armies and Fortifications of the Hundred Years War* (paperback edn, Boydell Press, 1999).

For general accounts of the evolution of early plate armour in Europe see the old, but still excellent, summary by Claude Blair, *European Armour circa 1066 to circa 1700* (Batsford, 1959) and by David Edge and John Paddock, *The Armour of the Medieval Knight* (Bison Books, 1988). More recent research is represented by Tobias Capwell, "The English style: Armour Design in England 1400–1500" (PhD thesis, University of Leeds, 2004) and *Armour of the English Knight 1400–1450* (Thomas del Mar in association with Sotheby's, 2015); and Thom Richardson, "Armour in England, 1325–99", *Journal of Medieval History*, 37 (2011), 304–20, and "The Medieval Inventories of the Tower Armouries 1320–1410" (PhD thesis, University of York, 2012).

For archery, see M. Strickland and R. Hardy, *The Great Warbow. From Hastings to the Mary Rose* (Sutton Publishing, 2005), Alex Hildred (ed.) *Weapons of warre: the Armaments of the Mary Rose* (2011) with its full bibliography, Richard Wadge, *Arrowstorm. The World of the Archer in the Hundred Years War* (Spellmount, 2009), and for arrows, O. Jessop, "A New Artefact Typology for the Study of Medieval Arrowheads", *Medieval Archaeology*, 40 (1996), 192–205.

For edged weapons, Michael Coe et al, *Swords and Hilt Weapons* (London, 1989), Ewart Oakeshott, *The Sword in the Age of Chivalry* (London, 1964) and *Records of the European Sword* (Boydell Press, 1991) give the basic background. Other close combat weapons are less well served; see Kelly DeVries and Robert D. Smith, *Medieval Military Technology* (2nd edn, University of Toronto Press, 2012) for a survey. This work also includes a consideration of guns. The most comprehensive text on English firearms in the Middle Ages is by Howard Blackmore,

*The Armouries of the Tower of London* (H.M.S.O, 1976), with important European comparisons by Robert Smith and Kelly D Vries in *The Artillery of the Dukes of Burgundy 1363–1477* (Boydell Press, 2005). See also Sean McLachlan, *Medieval Handgonnes* (Osprey, 2010).

# ABOUT THE AUTHORS

The four authors of this book contributed text as follows: Anne Curry (Chapter 2); Anne Curry and Dan Spencer (Chapters 3, 4, 8, 9 and 14); Anne Curry, Peter Hoskins and Dan Spencer (Chapter 7); Peter Hoskins (Chapters 5 and 6); Thom Richardson (Chapters 11 and 12); Dan Spencer (Chapters 1, 10 and 13).

Anne Curry is Professor of Medieval History and Dean of the Faculty of Humanities at the University of Southampton. Her publications include *The Hundred Years War*, *The Battle of Agincourt: Sources and Interpretations*, *Agincourt: A New History*, *Great Battles: Agincourt*, *Henry V* in the Penguin Monarchs series, and (with Glenn Foard) *Bosworth: A Battlefield Rediscovered*. She is co-director of *www.medievalsoldier.org*, a Trustee of the Royal Armouries and Chair of Trustees of the Agincourt 600 charity.

Peter Hoskins is a former Royal Air Force pilot with an interest in the history of the Hundred Years War. He lives in France and has followed the itineraries of the Crécy, Poitiers and Agincourt campaigns on foot. He is the author of *In the Steps of the Black Prince, The Road to Poitiers 1355–1356* and, with Anne Curry, *Agincourt 1415: A Tourist's Guide to the Campaign*. A tourist guide to the Crécy campaign is forthcoming.

Thom Richardson is Deputy Master at the Royal Armouries, based in the Tower of London and Leeds. Having previously worked for the British Museum and Manchester City Art Gallery, he joined the staff of the Royal Armouries in 1984 and was Keeper of Armour and Oriental Collections until 2014. He has a PhD from the University of York on the records of the armouries of late medieval English kings at the Tower of London and is author of numerous books and articles on European and Asian arms and armour, including *The Medieval Armour from Rhodes, London Armourers in the 17th century* and *Littlecote House: the English Civil War Armoury.*

Dan Spencer is a doctoral candidate at the University of Southampton whose research investigates the development of English gunpowder artillery in the fifteenth century. He took his BA at the University of Exeter and his MA at the University of Southampton. His publications include articles on Bodiam and Roxburgh castles, as well as the use of firearms in the Hundred Years War and the Wars of the Roses. He also works on the Agincourt 600 project, *www.agincourt600.com.*

# OTHER TITLES IN THIS SERIES INCLUDE:

**The Tudor Treasury**
*A collection of fascinating facts and insights about the Tudor dynasty*
*Elizabeth Norton*
*9780233004334*

**Magna Carta and All That**
*A guide to the Magna Carta and life in England in 1215*
*Rod Green*
*9780233004648*

**The Victorian Treasury**
*A collection of fascinating facts and insights about the Victorian era*
*Lucinda Hawksley*
*9780233004778*